I Love Him L
He's Not a Cl

The Christian Woman's Guide to Deliverance from Toxic Relationships

Latasha G. Hines

Revised Edition

**Jewel
Publishers**

Jewel Publishers, LLC
P.O. Box 278006
Miramar, Florida 33027
www.jewelpublishers.com
(954) 432-0350

I Love Him Lord,^{TM} *but He's Not a Christian:*
The Christian Woman's Guide to
Deliverance from Toxic Relationships

Jewel Publishers, LLC
P.O. Box 278006
Miramar, Florida 33027
www.jewelpublishers.com

Library of Congress Control Number: 2007921434
ISBN-13: 978-0-9778322-1-7
ISBN-10: 0-9778322-1-X

Cover Creation and Design by Melvin Duerson

Printed in the United States of America

About the Author

A native Miamian, Latasha Gethers Hines lives in South Florida with her husband Travis, a real estate investor and sales agent. She has a stepdaughter, Teylor.

Latasha uses the Word of God to encourage people to embrace abundant life through Jesus Christ and use their talents to bless others and the Kingdom of God. An anointed teacher of God's Word, Latasha travels, sharing her powerful message of faith and deliverance with Bible study groups, book clubs, civic groups, and churches.

In 1994, Latasha earned a Bachelor of Science degree in journalism and a minor in speech communication from the University of Florida where she is a member of the Student Hall of Fame. She earned a Juris Doctor degree in 1997 from the University of Miami School of Law, where she graduated *cum laude*. For six and a half years, she practiced commercial litigation in private law firms in Miami, Florida, representing large corporations in business disputes.

In 2004, Latasha left private practice to pursue her lifelong love of writing and public speaking on Bible principles. She continues to write and speak on Bible principles, operate her own legal practice (specializing in business and real estate consulting), and volunteer with civic and professional organizations. Latasha is one of the founders of Voices of Prayer and Praise, a home-based women's Bible study group that began in 2000.

Dedication

I dedicate this book to the memory of my beloved grandmother, the late Bessie Mae Clark, from whom I learned perseverance; Travis Hines, my Spirit-filled true love; my sister-friends who encouraged me to trust God; and Roshonda Exantus, my little sister who shall do mighty exploits for God.

Acknowledgements

I honor my triune God—God the Father; God the Son, Jesus Christ; and God the Holy Spirit—for trusting the fallible me with this message for His daughters.

I respect and honor my husband, Travis Hines, for loving me as Christ loves the Church.

Much love is offered to my mother, Martha (Jewel) Clark Davis, for giving me life and for the sacrificial love of raising me as a single parent. Travis and I named our publishing company, Jewel Publishers, in honor of you.

I acknowledge Minister Irene Murph, my beloved aunt, for her insightful and Spirit-led assistance with *I Love Him Lord, but He's Not a Christian*. My grandmother's sacrificial spirit lives on in you.

I acknowledge my brother Andrew Gethers for his role in bringing Travis and me into each other's lives and supporting our endeavors. To my big sister Mary Simpson, thank you for always being there and loving me unconditionally.

To our prayer partners, friends, confidants, and supporters, Solomon and Sharon Nixon, Travis and I love you dearly for your unwavering partnership.

I honor the sisters of Voices of Prayer and Praise and my spiritual mother Jacqueline Johnson for nurturing my spiritual growth. Mama Jackie, your tough love means so much to me.

I honor my pastor, Wayne Lomax of The Fountain Ministries, and my former pastor, the late Nathan H. Pope, for feeding me the Word of Life.

Contents

Part III – Understand Your Value to God

Part IV – Engage in Spiritual Warfare

Part V – Commune with Your God

Part VI – Embrace Your Freedom

Foreword

A few months after I met Latasha in December of 2001, she shared with me the vision God gave her for a book to help Christian women get out of bad relationships. Latasha explained that the book was based on her journey toward deliverance from toxic relationships with men who were not Christians. Having known from the moment I met her that she would be my wife, I became determined to support her efforts to birth *I Love Him Lord, but He's Not a Christian*. I realized that her deliverance from toxic relationships opened the door to the life we now share.

Follow God's plan to deliver you from toxic relationships. *I Love Him Lord, but He's Not a Christian* is a powerful and anointed message that will set you free if you embrace its truths. As you yield to this message, allow God to examine your heart, deliver you from toxic relationships, and prepare you to be presented to your future husband. On these pages, you will find the healing and deliverance you need to understand that no man can love you as Jesus Christ loves the church unless he knows how Jesus Christ loves the church.

My wife is truly a beautiful vessel of God who has revealed her past to help women around the world have a better future. I am thankful that God delivered her from toxic relationships and pray that He will do the same for you.

Travis Hines

Foreword

Some challenges are only for the purely coura-geous. Orville and Wilbur Wright demonstrated such courage as aviation pioneers. Harriett Tubman's courage led hundreds of slaves from the brutality of the south to the beatific possibilities of freedom. Latasha has demonstrated literary courage by pen-ning, *I Love Him Lord, but He's Not a Christian*. As the presses are pouring out pages on prosperity, abun-dance, and being the best you can be, we are blind-sided by a dose of refreshing transparency that is punctuated with brutal honesty.

The text forces us to reflect on many of the possi-ble outcomes of dating a spiritually incompatible person. It is more than a warning, it is explanation and encouragement. In a world where relationships are becoming increasingly more complex, caused by the total secularization of the culture, the huge numbers of men in prison, the disproportionate number of female professionals, and the rise in the acceptance of alternative sexual lifestyles, Latasha calls us to make choices that reflect faithfulness and old school holiness.

Never harsh, never condemning, never holier than the reader, the text is a brilliant facet in the diamond of truth. *I Love Him Lord, but He's Not a Christian* prepares us to place our priority in the God who loves us more than all of the others who love us. And the God we love must be known by the person with whom we fall in love. If you like a challenge—keep turning the pages.

Pastor Wayne Lomax
The Fountain Ministries

Introduction

My college prayer partner was the type of person who often shared the details of her personal struggles with others. "Girl, why do you always tell people *your* business?" I asked. "It's not my business; it's God's business," she responded. Sharing her struggles in the context of sharing how God caused her to triumph over those struggles was an effective ministry tool. Her life's affairs were God's business.

I Love Him Lord, but He's Not a Christian was birthed out of my past personal struggles. I professed my uncompromising love for Jesus Christ to a man who was not a Christian, believing that my bold confession would establish the rules of our courtship. Although he did not believe in my God, I thought that my strong belief would win the struggle over his unbelief. His equally strong renouncement—"I will never be a Christian"—did not deter my involvement with him because he was such a "nice guy." I was convinced that he would change. During that time, he did not change. I changed. I found myself professing that Jesus was the light of my life, yet walking in darkness. Through my actions, I opened my entire being to toxins that could have destroyed me.

Many of us have settled for toxic relationships, buying into the notion that it is better to have someone than exist alone. You are probably like I once was, being courted by men whom you know are not Christians, yet you believe in God for their salvation, with holy matrimony as the ultimate goal. You may even be in a relationship with a man who mirrors your response to the things of God, but without his own personal relationship with God, such a man can only mimic your behavior.

As Christians, oftentimes we know what is right. However, finding strength to do the right thing is a different story. Therefore, I write this book to share God's response to my cry, "I love him Lord, but he's not a Christian." This book is a tool to help guide unmarried Christian women through deliverance from toxic relationships. The Holy Scriptures support the fact that God desires His daughters to exist in healthy relationships, free of the toxins that seek to hinder us from enjoying the abundant life God ordained for us. *I am come that they might have life, and that they might have it more abundantly* (John 10:10).

Unequally yoked relationships, whether you are involved with someone who is not saved or someone who is immature in his relationship with Jesus Christ, will result in toxic relationships. Thus, God's admonition against attachments with unbelievers is the guiding law for the unmarried Christian woman's deliverance from toxic relationships. *Be ye not unequally yoked together with unbelievers: for what fellowship hath righteousness with unrighteousness? and what communion hath light with darkness?* (2 Corinthians 6:14).

I recognize that some of our Christian sisters have found themselves in toxic marriages. The Word of God instructs the Christian spouse to stay in that marriage and win the unsaved mate over with gentleness (1 Peter 3:1–5). God honors the Christian woman's submission to her husband, so long as he does not require her to do something in violation of God's Word. *Wives, submit yourselves unto your own husbands, as it is fit in the Lord* (Colossians 3:18). Sisters, the submission instruction is for wives. The marriage covenant that God modeled after His covenant with the church requires sacrifices unlike those in other relationships. The Holy Scriptures shared in this book pave the way for your deliverance from toxic relationships with unbelievers *prior to* marriage.

The toxin-free relationship I encourage in *I Love Him Lord, but He's Not a Christian* is a relationship between a Christian man and Christian woman in which the couple seeks God's will concerning whether they are to enter into a marriage covenant. The relationship to which I refer is not casual dating, but dating to gather information to determine whether the individual is the person you are to marry. Jesus Christ must be the basis for the toxin-free relationship.

I Love Him Lord, but He's Not a Christian encourages you, through God's Word, to seek freedom from the toxic relationship you may be in, forsake the toxic relationship you may be considering, or thwart the plan of the enemy to engage you in toxic relationships in the future. Many Christian women open their hearts to toxic relationships, creating voids that can only be filled through obedience to God's Word. If this is your situation, I encourage you to allow God the Father; God the Son, Jesus Christ; and God the Holy Spirit to fill the missing pieces in your heart as you journey toward the equally yoked relationship God ordained for you.

This book also is a guide designed to help believers empower their friends and loved ones to ward off and get out of toxic relationships. Allow God to use you to hold fellow believers accountable for their relationships with God.

Although this book is addressed to my fellow Christian sisters, it is a message for my Christian brothers as well. God hears your cry: "I love her Lord, but she's not a Christian." Unarguably, you face many of the same challenges created by toxic relationships. The dominating male ego may convince you that you have the power to change a woman. Oftentimes, it is you who is changed, all in the pursuit of a woman's outer deceitful beauty. *Favour is deceitful, and beauty is vain: but a woman that feareth the LORD, she shall be praised* (Proverbs 31:30). I challenge you, my Christian brothers, to preserve yourselves for a woman who fears the Lord. The beauty of the woman who fears God exudes from the inside out.

Married men and women will also benefit from the Bible principles taught in *I Love Him Lord, but He's Not a Christian*. Married men, be reminded of the great responsibility you have as Christian husbands – sacrificially love your wife as Christ loves the church. Be mighty men of God, distinct from worldly men, and be renewed in your commitment to a Godly marriage.

Married women in equally yoked unions should remember the blessing of existing in a union ordained by God. *I Love Him Lord, but He's Not a Christian* will help you understand how valuable you are to God and be encouraged to be a mighty woman of

God, worthy of God's very best. For Christian married women whose husbands fall short of loving them as Christ loves the church, this book will encourage you to pray for your husband so that you can enjoy the benefit of the love God intended for you to have.

I Love Him Lord, but He's Not a Christian will help us all embrace the abundant life God has for us in our relationships.

PART I

Decipher the Relationship

Chapter One

What is Love?

> For God so loved the world, that he gave his only
> begotten Son, that whosoever believeth in him
> should not perish, but have everlasting life.
> John 3:16

Love means different things to people at different stages of their lives. As young children, we love teddy bears and ice cream. Some young adults direct their love toward friends, fashion, and superstars. At some point, in the quest for a relationship, many young women direct their love toward a man. As a Christian woman, you must be certain that the love you direct toward a man is rooted in the Word of God.

"I love him. Yes, Lord, I really do love him." I hear

your heart beating this declaration. "This incredible longing to help this man reach his best in life and to have him erase loneliness from my life, must originate from love," I hear the cymbals of your heart clang. Yet, the Word of God warns us that the heart is deceitful and desperately wicked (Jeremiah 17:9). The enemy infiltrates hearts that are not completely yielded to God.

The heart is our spiritual center, but sin can cause it to rise up and act as our emotional center. As the spiritual center, it is the place where we first connect with God. The heart is the place where the manifestation of our adoption into the kingdom of God is birthed. Although others can see and hear our confession of faith in Jesus, only God knows whether our confession is genuine. When our confession is genuine, a changed heart is created, and salvation is the result.

However, when we replace the truth of God's Word with self, emotions spill over into our hearts, deceiving us of the truth. Thus, deceitfully wicked thoughts and actions move in to set our courses. A course established by a heart of deceitfully wicked thoughts and actions is bound for destruction. Therefore, we must yield our total existence to the leading of the Holy Spirit. We must allow the Holy Spirit to search our hearts and reveal to us the deceptions of the enemy.

Proverbs 4:23 reveals that out of the heart flows the issues of life. So what is flowing out of your heart? Is it God's truth regarding love or Satan's deception regarding love? We must replace the world's love standards with God's standards for love. God's truth regarding love is made clear in His Word. Many different expressions of love are identified in the Word of God. Here, we will explore three of the love expressions identified in God's Word—philadelphia, agape, and philandros.

The Greek word "filadelfiva," translated "philadelphia," is brotherly love shown among believers. This love is expressed in 1 Peter 1:22: *Seeing ye have purified your souls in obeying the truth through the Spirit unto unfeigned love of the brethren, see that ye love one another with a pure heart fervently.* This passage talks about a genuine love for the brethren. It is born out of a common interest—Jesus Christ. One who loves Jesus is drawn to others who love Jesus. The God in us loves the God in others. This type of love gives no place to lust or selfish desires. Brotherly love has no hidden agenda. It is expressed from the depth of a pure heart that bears witness to the Spirit of God operating in the lives of the brethren.

Brotherly love is the type of love that is often confused if you set on a course of missionary dating. Missionary dating occurs when a Christian dates someone who is unsaved with the purpose of converting him to Christ. The desire for the unsaved person's conversion is premised on the hope that he will be your husband. However, the sincere and true desire should be that he unites with God, even if he will become someone else's husband.

As Christians, we should desire that all of mankind come to the saving knowledge of Jesus Christ. In fact, we are commissioned as followers of Christ to share the gospel with unbelievers that they may also enjoy the inheritance we have in Christ Jesus (Mark 16:15). We must share the gospel from a pure heart. God uses us in different ways to minister to the lost. Some of us are seed planters, sharing the simple message of God's love. Others of us are responsible for watering the Word, teaching and encouraging the lost to live for God. We must allow God to dictate the role we play in our encounters with unbelievers.

We must share the Good News with those whom the Lord places on our paths. We do not always get the reward of being there at the moment they invite Jesus Christ into their hearts, but our witness may have been what pointed them in the direction of God. Of course, you should share your faith as the Holy Spirit leads you with the non-believing object of your desire. But the sharing should be limited to the sharing of the salvation message. The work of growing him up in the things of God is best reserved for the church or other unattached believers. In fact, he can learn more about the power of God by watching you live a life that is devoted to God—a life that is consistent with the Christ in whom you believe.

When your devotion to God is distracted, the door to your spiritual being opens to confusion from the enemy. Is this brother truly seeking a personal relationship with God, or is he doing whatever it takes to maintain his position with you? He must desire a relationship with God independent of you. God must be his first love, evidenced through his commitment to study, pray, worship, and live for Christ Jesus.

Are you sowing into his life out of a heart of genuine sisterly love for the salvation of the lost or is it out of a deceitful heart set on making him suitable for marriage? Consider your intentions. What if God desires to use you to share the gospel with him, facilitating his growth into a mighty man of God who will love, nurture, and support *another woman.* You must have a genuine desire for his salvation.

God loves him more than you are capable of loving him. Whether he is an unbeliever or immature in his relationship with God, you must know that his salvation and relationship with God is more important than anything else. His life is at stake. Prayerfully yield your desires to have him as a mate to God's desire to have him as a son. Share the plan of salvation with him and direct him to someone who can help him mature spiritually. Pray for him.

Nancy pursued a relationship with Fred under the guise of teaching him about Jesus. She was very attracted to him from the first time she saw him moving into her apartment complex. After several cordial exchanges, Nancy asked Fred whether he was interested in attending a local play with her. He declined.

During a church service, Nancy's pastor challenged the congregation to share the gospel with someone. She decided that the pastor's challenge presented an opportunity for her to interact with Fred.

She shared her faith with him one day and he responded with excitement. Fred became very curious about the life of Jesus and the promise of salvation. He attended bible study sessions at her church. He called her often for prayer and to discuss scriptures. She was so pleased to be spending time with him at church and talking with him on the telephone. She searched for neighborhood bible study groups, hoping to capitalize on his growing love for God by spending more time with him at the bible study meetings.

She was distraught when he responded to the pastor's invitation to accept Jesus Christ as Lord and Savior, with another woman standing by his side—the woman he planned to marry. Rather than celebrate his entry into eternal life with the Lord, she lamented over the fact that she had invested so much time in his spiritual growth to make him a good husband for someone else.

Allow the Holy Spirit to search your heart. He will reveal whether you are truly operating in the philadelphia type of love.

The Greek word "ajgavph," translated "agape," is the sacrificial love best demonstrated by Jesus. This love is expressed in Romans 5:8: *But God commendeth his love toward us, in that, while we were yet sinners, Christ died for us.* Even in our filthy state of sin, God's agape love pardoned our sins, and He accepted death that was rightfully ours. God's agape love is extended to the sinner and the believer. God backed up His love by offering His only begotten Son to death on a cross. That is a strong expression of love. God's requirement that a husband love his wife as Christ loves the church is a call to the agape expression of love.

Embrace God's love, prior to directing your affections toward a person. You must know that God loves you so very much and that He made you whole and complete in Him. God must be your first love. How can you demonstrate the love God has for you to a husband if you do not love God, your Creator. Your life is in God's hands. Is a person more worthy of love than the God who created you and gives you life? You must get to the place where God truly is sufficient and you are content in Him before you are capable of sharing your love with a man. Embrace God's love (Ephesians 3:17-19). When you embrace the love God has for you, your eyes will open to the type of love that is expected from a man who wants a relationship with you. The Lord sets the standard for love.

Then there is the Greek word "fivlandroß," translated "philandros," which expresses the love a wife has for her husband. Titus 2:4–5 reads: *That they may teach the young women to be sober, to love their husbands, to love their children, To be discreet, chaste, keepers at home, good, obedient to their own husbands, that the word of God be not blasphemed.*

There is an extreme level of devotion required to exhibit the love a wife should have for her husband. It is devotion through the good, bad, and disappointing times of life. This devotion is born out of the marriage covenant—a covenant that models the covenant Christ has with his church. It is a covenant of unconditional love in action. It is a covenant of companionship. It is a ministry covenant. The marriage covenant is made of an enduring love, filled with passion and sacrifice. A wife's failure to operate in the level of love required of a wife toward her husband is deemed blasphemy to God's Word (Titus 2:4–5).

As an unmarried woman, your attempt to love a man with the level of love required of a wife for her husband can lead to destruction. When you give the sacrificial love of a wife to a man, you give a part of yourself. Giving of yourself to one who is not committed to you in marriage leaves you vulnerable.

Many women find themselves "playing house" as they intertwine their lives with men who are not their husbands. Sex outside of marriage leaves you vulnerable because you give a precious part of yourself to someone who is not obligated to love you as Christ loves the church. Unions that involve fornication are contrary to God's Word.

In the book of Mark, marriage requirements are given: *But from the beginning of the creation God made them male and female. For this cause shall a man leave his father and mother, and cleave to his wife; And they twain shall be one flesh: so then they are no more twain, but one flesh. What therefore God hath joined together, let not man put asunder* (Mark 10: 6-9). The Word of God requires a man to leave his father and mother and bind himself to his wife, becoming one flesh with her. There is no such requirement when the man is just a boyfriend. He is not required to elevate you among others he loves—parents, siblings, and children. In a marriage, spouses should be regarded above all other people, second only to God.

A woman who tries to unite with a man who is not her husband is at risk of giving too much of herself without receiving the benefits of the martial union. Why risk "playing house" with someone who does not have legal or spiritual obligations to you? Why risk your relationship with God by "playing house" with someone who is not committed to being one flesh with you?

When you unite with a man who is not your husband, you risk being vulnerable to a man who does not have the fear of the Lord for the consequences of how he treats his bride. God holds husbands accountable for honoring their wives. If a husband fails to honor his wife, his prayers to God are hindered (1 Peter 3:7). When you give a part of yourself to someone who is not accountable to God, you cannot be sure whether that person will forever embrace that part of you. Furthermore, you place yourself in a position to be used for his selfish desires. In some situations, he may, tragically, toss that part of you away.

I hear you saying that even in some Christian marriages there is no such assurance. You are right. But I am talking about marriages between men and women who are not only Christians in name, but Christians in deed—Christians who earnestly work to be in the will of the Father. Giving of yourself can be risky whether you are married or dating. However, the risks increase tremendously when you give a part of you that was intended for your God-fearing husband to a man who does not fear God.

Prayerful Application

Allow the Holy Spirit to search your heart and reveal the motives behind the love you are expressing to the man in your life.

Chapter Two

How to Detect Whether You Are in a Toxic Relationship

The heart is deceitful above all things, and desperately wicked: who can know it?
Jeremiah 17:9

"Toxic" is defined as "extremely harsh, malicious, or harmful." (*Merriam-Webster Online Dictionary*, 2007).

A toxic relationship is one that strips you of the ability to live a life that is pleasing to God. The toxins that enter your mind, spirit, and body destroy your balance. A toxic relationship poisons you and threatens to make you unreceptive to the voice of God.

Rather than accept the Word of God as truth, the toxins that fill your mind, spirit, and body cause you to justify your decision to live contrary to God's laws.

In your mind, you reason that because you believe you love him and he loves you, it is enough to sustain the relationship. But the Word of God cautions us to not be unequally yoked with unbelievers (2 Corinthians 6:14). When you yoke yourself with someone, you are bound to him. You take on his ways. You become one with him. Being yoked with the wrong person can cause devastation in your life.

If you are not careful, rather than being strengthened and encouraged in the pursuit of the things of God, a toxic relationship can lead your spirit away from the things of God. Often, the leading away of your spirit occurs in seemingly harmless stages. You accept his invitation to dinner on Wednesday night when you should be in Bible class. You accept his invitation to spend "special time" together for Sunday morning brunch when you should be feasting on the Word of God in Sunday service. You engage in late night telephone calls that last well into the early hours of the morning, and then drift off into sleep, failing to bow and give thanks to the Father. It all seems so wonderful. His intent in showering you with this goodness is to show his love for you. In many instances, there is no malice.

However, these behaviors are toxic, eating away at your spiritual development. You become imbalanced. Rather than preserving your body as the temple of the Holy Ghost (1 Corinthians 6:19), you open the door to toxic influences that methodically engulf you. The mission of toxic influences is to steal you from the Kingdom of God, kill the future plans God has for you, and destroy your faith in God. Do not allow toxic relationships to trap you. You were created for God's glory (Isaiah 43:7). God has plans to prosper you and give you good success (Joshua 1:8).

Toxic relationships interfere with God's plans. Such relationships can weigh you down, preventing you from blossoming into the woman of God our Creator envisioned of you. We have a loving Father who forgives us of our sins when He looks upon the blood of Jesus Christ. Yet our decisions set things into motion that create consequences we are forced to live with forever. Do not allow toxic relationships to take you off the course God designed for you.

There was a young woman who was reared in a Christian family. She established a relationship with Jesus Christ early in her life. She met a young man who lived a life far from the things of God. During their initial lunch meeting, she talked and talked and talked. He listened. She told him about her love of God, her major involvement in her church and the love her family had for God. She told him how she dreamed of marrying a man who loved God as much as she did. She told him the things she liked in a man.

He listened to all that she had to say and began to transform outwardly into the person she described. Yet his dark heart was far from the image he portrayed. After much prodding, he attended church service with her occasionally. He courted her relentlessly. Although he attended Sunday church service with her occasionally, he refused to participate in other church activities or to attend any gatherings with her family or friends.

After several months of dating, he asked her to marry him. She was thrilled with the offer but torn over the fact that he had not declared Jesus Christ as his Lord and Savior. She began to push him concerning the things of God, praying with him and for him continuously, consistently telling him about the salvation offered through Jesus Christ. While rejecting her God, he convinced her that she should not allow their beliefs to separate them.

She married him to the disapproval of her friends, family, and the Holy Spirit, who cautioned her from within. Months into her marriage, her husband took off his mask and allowed his true nature to surface. He abused her physically and emotionally. Yet she remained in that marriage and did not tell anyone except her God about the abuse she suffered because she remembered her vow, "until death do we part." He isolated her from her family, friends, and even her church.

They conceived children—two girls and a boy. Their family grew, adding two granddaughters and one grandson. Both generations witnessed the physical and verbal abuse, but they discussed it with no one but themselves. The children and even the grandchildren begged her to leave their abusive father and grandfather. Yet she resolved herself to the belief that she was getting what she deserved and that she should not expect anything better.

Her marriage established a course that impacts generations today. Their daughters never married for the fear of being locked into an abusive relationship.

One daughter had three children with three different fathers. The second daughter refused to have children. The son married and abused his wife because he loved her, he explained as he lavished her with physical and verbal assaults. Then the grandchildren continued down the toxic road. One granddaughter, like her mother, bore three children with three different fathers. The second granddaughter married but refused to bring a life into the world for fear that her child could someday be abused or become an abuser. The grandson married four times and fathered seven children. There was a generational curse running its course, leaving destruction behind.

Indeed, we are all accountable for our individual actions. Just because people are born into a certain environment does not mean that their lives will be plagued by the events of that environment. The delivering power of Jesus Christ is strong enough to overpower any generational curse. However, some families have been unable to escape generational curses. The seed took root when mama first said "yes" to a man to whom the Holy Spirit warned her to say "no".

Relationships must be premised on the Word of God. When the beliefs and practices of the unbeliever negatively impact your relationship with God, the relationship is toxic. It becomes toxic when the Christian becomes emotionally attached to the unbeliever, giving way to pleasing the flesh and forsaking holy and righteous living.

When navigating new encounters with men, we often find ourselves struggling to assess the purpose for which the men have been sent into our lives. Indeed, it is possible that the unsaved brother who crosses your path is your future husband. But it is also possible that the season for the revelation that he is your husband has not yet arrived. Until God reveals him as your husband, do not alter your course in the pursuit of a relationship. You must guard your heart against engaging in a relationship that could become toxic or continuing to engage in one that is already toxic. God saves people—not you. Therefore, until a man accepts God's invitation to eternal life and matures in Christ, you should not commit to a relationship with him.

There's the possibility that the man, whether he is a Christian or not, is in your life to be a friend or an associate. Enjoy the gift of friendship or association without trying to turn it into something more. Do not discard friends of the opposite sex merely because they are not saved. Approach such friends with the brotherly love intended for all mankind. But in doing so, do not fool yourself into believing that you are exercising brotherly love when you know the emotional part of you is longing for something more. Even in situations where the man is a believer, he may not have matured in his relationship with Christ.

It is important that your interaction with him does not ruin your witness for Christ. God wants to use you to exemplify what it means to walk with God. We must not only say what we believe, but we must live what we believe before others so that they can see the genuine love that we have for God and ultimately long to express that same love to God.

Do not get distracted in your walk with God because of the hope for a life-long mate. Stay the course with God and obey His Word so that you can enjoy the fruit of a true relationship established by God. Only God knows whether the brother will accept Jesus as Lord and Savior. Therefore, you must protect yourself against what the Bible calls a deceitful and desperately wicked heart (Jeremiah 17:9).

Time reveals the true heart of a man. Therefore, new encounters should be tested with patience and prayer.

As I look back over my journals from my early twenties, I shudder as I read my accounts of what I thought were relationships that God had destined for marriage. The words on the pages of my journals were written with such emotion as I expressed the belief that I had met the man who was destined to be my husband, not once but twice. It did not matter that one did not produce the fruit of one who truly lives for God. The fact that he said he went to church seemed sufficient, even though he never went with me. It did not matter that one man outright denied that Jesus was the Messiah. Surely he would acknowledge someday soon that Jesus is the one through whom we receive salvation and the promise of eternal life, I reasoned.

The words on the pages of those journals were written with such conviction and in what I believed was faith. It was "faith" powered by my deceitful heart. It was "faith" born out of childhood Cinderella dreams of a fairytale wedding. My wicked heart convinced me that my prince charming had arrived, not once but twice. I believed it because I felt it in my heart.

By the time my husband showed up in my life, I had learned to test my heart-felt feelings with the Word of God to ward off counterfeit feelings. I, like many young women, desired to be married in my twenties. I figured that after going to college, then law school, and obtaining a great job in a top law firm, a husband was the next "thing" to acquire. Since I was in acquisition mode, I evaluated most men that I met based on the criteria I had established for the acquisition of a husband. Tall (a must), handsome (strongly preferred), professional (expected), and a believer in Jesus, as Lord and Savior (required, so I told myself). As I sought to obtain the next status level in life—-wife—-I began to entertain men who did not fit the criteria, because after all, I had an acquisition to complete.

I convinced myself that because I had petitioned God and given him my demands for the type of husband I wanted, the men who showed up in my life had to have been sent by God. Three out of five did not seem like such bad odds. This must be love, I reasoned without asking God for his input. It had a snowball effect. I reasoned: "I prayed. God heard me. This guy shows up with three out of the five things I requested. It's nice to have a companion to escort me to couples events. Everyone else is getting married. I desire to marry. I love him. Yes, I love him. That settles it—-I'll broker the deal and finalize the acquisition."

On my journey, I came face to face with the Word of God in Proverbs 18:22: *Whoso findeth a wife findeth a good thing, and obtaineth favour of the Lord.* I began to understand that God did not intend for me to find a husband, but that I had to be found by him. My job was to strive toward living in a way that pleased God and brought Him glory. The counterfeit feelings of love that crept up when I dated outside of the will of God, did not have a hold on me. By the time I met Travis, I had stopped looking. When he appeared in my life, I did not run down my check list. I did not consider whether he was a possible acquisition.

In fact, my journals from the days of my friendship with my husband indicate that I believed that his sole purpose in my life was to be just a friend. In response to my question to God about Travis' purpose in my life, I heard in my spirit that I was to be a friend to Travis and allow my life to lead him back to a strong relationship with the Lord. (Travis revealed to me that he had strayed away from God because of a pastor's deceitful actions toward him.)

It wasn't until a few months before he asked me to marry him that the Lord revealed to me that he was my husband. God knew that He had to complete a work in Travis, my friend, before He presented him as my husband. Also, God knew that I could not handle knowing early on in the friendship that Travis was my husband. Perhaps that knowledge would have made it difficult for us to truly commit to the friendship that formed the basis for our marriage.

Do not allow toxic relationships designed by Satan to distract you in your pursuit of living a victorious life as a follower of Christ. Size up every relationship or potential relationship with the Word of God to protect you from the trap of a toxic relationship.

The Word of God cautions us against uniting with

unbelievers (2 Corinthians 6:14). Is he a believer in Jesus Christ? Does he have a mature relationship with the Lord? Do you have a mature relationship with the Lord? Do you have a mutual desire to serve God and live according to His laws, with Jesus as your example?

As you spend time with God asking him for a mate or for insight concerning the relationship you are in, be open to hear God's response. God knows the heart of a man as well as yours. What appears on the surface is not always real; therefore, test it with the Word of God.

Prayerful Application

Ask God to show you the heart of the man with whom you are involved or with whom you are contemplating a relationship. Ask God to define his role in your life. Receive the revelation imparted unto you concerning him.

Chapter Three

How Did You Get to This Point?

> *I was not in safety, neither had I rest,*
> *neither was I quiet; yet trouble came.*
> Job 3:26

W e arrive at different stages of our lives at different paces. We approach some of those periods deliberately and reflectively, allowing the hand of God to guide us step by step as we follow with hearts and ears attuned to hear His voice. Then there are some stages that we reach so quickly, moving at such supersonic speed that everything in our path is a blur. The supersonic speed halts when we hit the brick wall that prevents us from moving forward and causes us to question how we reached this place.

You may have taken the bait that has enticed you into a relationship with a non-Christian. All too often, it begins with spending time with a man because he is a "nice guy." After investing so much time in the relationship, you find it hard to walk away. You hold on in "faith," hoping that the brother will change. You may even marry him, hoping he will change. Then you wake up one day and realize that you do not have God's very best for you. Unfortunately, when tough times show up and you need spiritual support, he cannot provide it. Now you understand that he's not God's very best because he is unable to provide the spiritual support you need. Your arrival at this point in life has everything to do with the choices you have made.

Without beating up on yourself, you have to acknowledge the role you played in allowing yourself to get entangled in a toxic relationship. Before you shift a portion of the blame to someone else, you must come to terms with the mistakes you may have made that rendered you vulnerable to the trappings of a toxic relationship. In most instances, God wants to teach you something about yourself through the experience. Did you forsake the warnings of those closest to you? Did you reject the inner witness of the Holy Spirit warning you not to proceed? Was he just a master deceiver, going undetected by your internal radar? Did you invite the toxic relationship through your behavior?

We must ask the Holy Spirit to search our hearts and reveal anything in us that is in opposition to God. The Holy Spirit must do the revealing. When we search ourselves, we are prone to gloss over areas of our lives that we're not ready to address. When the

Holy Spirit shines the light on our lives, our sins become glaring, highlighting the need to repent and live in a way that pleases God.

Tina complained constantly about the sexual advances men made toward her. After all, she was a Christian woman who dedicated her life to the things of God. She was really disturbed by the constant sexual advances. The men she met often made sexual advances toward her quickly, sometimes upon the initial meeting. She attracted these men in all sorts of environments, including evening social gatherings, work, children's events, business meetings, and even church. "Why me?" she questioned. Her conclusion was that all men are dogs.

One day, Tina cried out to a dear male friend, Robert, about her frustration with men making sexual advances toward her. Robert, a Christian with whom she had a platonic relationship, shared with her that he, too, had struggled with a sexual attraction toward her when they first met. He admitted that it took much prayer and even fasting to get beyond his sexual attraction for her and accept her as a friend and sister in the Lord. Tina was shocked at Robert's confession. She was hurt to know that even her dear friend had once looked upon her with sexual desire. "Why does this happen to me?" she asked.

Prayerfully, Robert explained. "It has a lot to do with the way you dress. There's no secret about what you have. You place your entire body on display. Therefore, men are drawn to what you are presenting—your flesh. Since you are presenting flesh, fleshly men are drawn to your flesh. It is hard for Christian men to break through the barrier of your flesh and get to know the true you because they assume that the true you is what's on display."

Tina realized that what she perceived as a sexy and sophisticated style was interpreted as revealing and enticing to men. She acknowledged that she had felt like the "ugly duckling" growing up and was always the subject of teasing by boys. Therefore, as an adult, she dressed provocatively to catch the attention of men, but she didn't want them to be attracted to her solely in a sexual way.

God used Tina's friend to illuminate an issue she had overlooked in her life. Tina talked to God about the way she dressed, the motives behind her choices, and the attention she attracted. She gained understanding as to the error of her ways, confessed her sins to God, and allowed the Holy Spirit to show her how to dress in a way that glorifies God.

Once you acknowledge that you share in the blame, it is time to receive the mercy and forgiveness that God promised us upon confession of our sins. Surely, God is faithful and just to forgive us of our sins (1 John 1:9). What is the sin? In most instances, it is the sin of disobedience—disobeying the Word of God that instructs us regarding the types of relationships that displease God. It is the sin of disobeying the inner witness of the Holy Spirit, who whispers, "Caution, daughter. Do not give him your heart. You cannot change him."

As you figure out how you got to this place in your relationship, learn from the experience so that you are better equipped to deal with similar tests that may come your way. The enemy uses relationships to tempt Christian single women into abandoning their course with God. The temptation is birthed in the flesh's desire and the lure of a relationship with a man they can see, feel, and touch. But remember that through prayer, our spiritual being can see, feel, and touch our God!

Even when the Father sends you that awesome man of God with whom you will share the joys and struggles of marriage, you will find that God is a better man than your spouse will ever be. Since God is the key to a life of joy, happiness, success, and fulfillment, now is the time to fall in love with Him. Allow Him to be your everything so that when the spouse God has chosen for you shows up, he is an added gift to your life and not the sole focus. God should forever be the main focus of your life. Live so that you please Him in all that you do and in all that you are.

Prayerful Application

In prayer, allow the Lord to reveal the sins concerning your relationship. Forgive yourself for falling into the trap of a toxic relationship. Confess your sins, forgive yourself, and allow God to heal and deliver you.

Part II

Face the Realities of
the Relationship

Chapter Four

How Can He Love You as Christ Loves the Church if He Does Not Know How Christ Loves the Church?

Husbands, love your wives, even as Christ also loved the church, and gave himself for it. So ought men to love their wives as their own bodies. He that loveth his wife loveth himself. For no man ever yet hated his own flesh; but nourisheth and cherisheth it, even as the Lord the church.
Ephesians 5:25, 28–29

All too often, we ask, even beg people to give us something they are incapable of giving. They are not

49

capable of giving it because they do not truly understand what we seek. So when you ask him for commitment, he reduces the list of women he is dating to two, giving you priority over the other woman. When you ask for love, he merely tells you he loves you without actions to back it up. You ask for emotional help; he opens his wallet. Although you are clear about that which you ask, the translation is lost in the delivery, precluding him from giving you what you want.

As a Christian woman in a toxic relationship, you may find yourself longing for love. Your mate may tell you that he loves you and give you things as expressions of love. However, that kind of "love" does not quite quench the Christian woman's thirst. It is because the love that we desire is a love modeled after Christ, a love that ministers to our spirits. *Husbands, love your wives, even as Christ also loved the church, and gave himself for it. So ought men to love their wives as their own bodies. He that loveth his wife loveth himself. For no man ever yet hated his own flesh; but nourisheth and cherisheth it, even as the Lord the church* (Ephesians 5:25, 28–29).

The ultimate love a husband expresses toward his wife should model the love Christ has for His church. Christ sacrificed so much so that we, His followers, could enjoy the benefits of eternity with the Father. A husband's love is to model Jesus' sacrifice. It is a love that is as deep as the love for himself. It is a love that drives him to nourish, provide for, protect, and strengthen his wife. He cherishes and adores her. He supports and encourages her. He protects and provides for her. He helps her be her very best.

This is the love for which most women thirst, whether they are Christians or not. The Christian woman gains understanding regarding the nature of her thirst through the Word of God. She wants what the Holy Bible says she is entitled to receive— sacrificial, nourishing love.

As a Christian woman, you will run into problems if you try to force a man who does not know God to love you as God loves him. The unbeliever does not know the nature of God and, therefore, has difficulty modeling the love of God. How can he love you as Christ loves the church if he does not know how Christ loves the Church? He cannot, which is why the longing for true love remains in your heart.

In some instances, you can experience what appears to be this sacrificial, nourishing love for a season. The question is whether it will endure through the challenges that come with a lifetime commitment. Often, it does not. Love does not endure unless it has been empowered to endure. We as Christians are empowered by the Holy Spirit to live out our lives on the earth. We allow the power of God to operate in our lives and compel us to move in the direction God has established for us. It is the inner witness of the Holy Spirit who corrects us, counsels us, and encourages us to live holy for God. The inner witness of the Holy Spirit also instructs us on how to relate with mankind. People who act without the guidance of the Holy Spirit are led by the powers of darkness. Indeed, they may have good morals and follow good life principles, but their goodness does not compare to God's greatness.

I saw the difference as I walked through two dark

periods in my life. The passing of my grandmother, who had helped my mom raise me, was a tough experience. As I walked through that tough season of watching her body submit to sickness and ultimately death, my friend could not minister to me. Although he was kind and considerate, visiting grandma in the hospital, sending flowers, offering words of comfort the best he knew how, it was not enough. He could not reach my spirit—the very part of me that needed encouraging.

A few years later, death knocked at the door of another loved one—my aunt Vivian. At that time, the man who would eventually be my husband was courting me. He was there when I got the call. My aunt had stopped breathing. As we raced to my aunt's house, my mind was blank with dread. But I heard a voice praying that she would live and not die, praying for peace and comfort, praying the power of God into the situation that awaited us. My aunt chose heaven that evening over a life of sickness here on earth.

The days to come were difficult, causing me to doubt my faith, albeit for only a short time. But my soon-to-be husband, whom God had allowed into my inner court to see the pain I experienced, prayed me through. His being there to hold my hand and embrace me through sobs was not enough to wrestle me from the grief I felt. It was during our time apart that he interceded for me, asking God to strengthen and comfort me. That intercession allowed me to receive the oil of joy for mourning (Isaiah 61:3).

It is in the darkest hours of our lives that relationships are tested. We need to know that our mates love us enough to wage war against the very enemy of our souls. Your potential husband need not only be willing to engage the enemy on your behalf, but he needs to be equipped for battle. The enemy targets strong Christian relationships. Satan knows that if he can destroy a marriage, he has a chance of impacting children, the church, and the community for generations to come. The enemy knows that if he can destroy a relationship that is destined for marriage, he has one less powerful team opposing him. Evenly yoked unions can withstand the attacks of Satan.

Christ loves His church so much that He sacrificed Himself so that we would be victorious against the devil. You want your lifelong mate to love you as Christ loves His church.

Prayerful Application

Pray and ask God to reveal to you whether the man in your life has accepted Jesus Christ as Lord and Savior. Then ask God if he is growing toward loving you as Christ loves the church.

Chapter Five

You Cannot Change Him, So Stop Trying!

For the people turneth not unto him that smiteth them, neither do they seek the LORD of hosts.
Isaiah 9:13

When you meet a man who has most of the qualities you are attracted to, it is easy to relegate his lack of a relationship with the Lord as that one small thing that can be changed. After all, he seems to measure up in so many other areas. Making your way through your checklist, you find yourself placing check after check after check—tall (check), handsome (check), intelligent (check), driven (check), successful (check), and solid family background (check). Then you reach the requirement that he must be a mature Christian. Because he has met all of the other requirements, surely you cannot give up on him for this one inadequacy, you reason. After all, he can change, you hope. I am woman enough to change him, you think. After all, I am a strong woman of God, you declare.

Just because that brother is not a follower of Jesus today does not mean he will not follow Jesus tomorrow; he may even become a mighty soul winner for the Kingdom of God. People are capable of change. If we were not capable of change, Jesus' death on the cross for our salvation would have been useless. We would have existed in a perpetual state of sin without the ability to evolve into repentant followers of Jesus. Indeed, he can change. But God is the only one who knows for sure whether the man will ever belong to Him. The Father is the only one who can change the heart of the man to draw him unto Himself. You are not God. You cannot change him, so stop trying!

The only person you can control is yourself. Your deliverance from the toxic relationship you may find yourself in is linked with your ability to understand that it is *you* who must change. If you fail to change your heart and mind concerning the toxic relationship, Satan will continue to deceive you as he sets you up for a big fall. If you are not careful, you will wake up one day and realize that while you focused your attention on changing your partner, you compromised your own values.

Diana experienced the reality of waking up one day and having it dawn on her that, indeed, she had changed in her quest to change Timothy, the man she wanted to marry. Diana met Timothy at the birthday party of a mutual friend. From the moment he walked through the door, she could not resist his deliberate stares in her direction. Diana had been divorced for five years, and her children were adults. She secretly applauded herself for having the ability to draw the attention of what she thought was the finest man at the birthday gathering, even though she was overweight. Eventually, Timothy made his way to her and introduced himself. She felt an immediate attraction to him.

He seemed to be just the kind of man she was looking for. He worked in the same industry as she did. (Check – "He makes a good living and has benefits," she thought.) He had a similar jovial personality. (Check – "I will not be embarrassed to take him to the company's Christmas party," she reasoned.) He gave up his home to live with his aging mother so that he could take care of her. (Check – "He is caring, loyal and responsible," she assumed.) He attended the well-known mega church in town, so he told her. (Check – "He is a Christian," she concluded.)

Diana prayed and asked God to show her whether Timothy was the one for her. Little by little, the stories Timothy told Diana the night he met her at the party did not check out. Indeed, Timothy worked in the same industry as she did, but it was later revealed that he had five different jobs in that industry over the past three years. He was fired from three of the five jobs. His ailing mother was sick because of the stress Timothy caused in her life. Although she was a widow, she was forced to work to take care of her basic needs because Timothy did not help with the home expenses. At the age of 50, Timothy had never owned his own home and lived with his mother between stints of living with other women. As for his church membership, there was no such record. The leader of the prayer ministry to which he claimed he belonged had never heard of him.

Although the deception was revealed, Diana believed that she could persuade him to pursue a relationship with the Lord. He just needed someone to love him and show him the way, she told herself. After all, she had already invested so much time in the relationship! Before long, she allowed Timothy to move into her home. He told her that he wanted to save money so that they could get married. It was a downward spiral from there. She began to forsake the things of God. In Diana's quest to change Timothy, she changed for the worse. Timothy's darkness dimmed God's light in her life.

It is important that we protect our relationship with God at all costs. We must not sacrifice our relationship with the Lord in our efforts to convince others to accept the God we love. In fact, our ability to live as committed Christians before nonbelievers can be effective in drawing them to the Lord. When we live for God, it shows that we are serious about our relationship with Him and that this relationship is supreme.

If you are contemplating engaging in a serious relationship with someone, he must know by your words, actions, and deeds that your relationship with God is important to you. You should live in such a way that your life exudes the importance of God. Nonbelievers are often discouraged when Christians talk about their love for God yet live in disobedience to God's instructions. As Christians, we must live with integrity so that we do not cause new Christians or nonbelievers to shun living for Christ. We must live what we preach.

Prayerful Application

Prayerfully describe your relationship with God prior to meeting the man in your life. How has your relationship with God changed? Allow the Holy Spirit to show you whether the efforts you have made to win the man to Christ have interfered with your personal relationship with Jesus Christ.

Chapter Six

Heartache and Destruction Are Inevitable

> *Be ye not unequally yoked together with unbelievers: for what fellowship hath righteousness with unrighteousness? And what communion hath light with darkness?*
> 2 Corinthians 6:14

When we make the decision to become followers of Jesus Christ, we should obey Him in all things, including relationships. God's Word forbids us from being unequally yoked; therefore, we must obey Him. Christians should become yoked in marriage with other believers. This divine covenant relationship then allows us to serve as witnesses to the world of the love Jesus has for His church. We are to allow God to yoke us in marriages with other believers who can help us become all that God wants us to be and

61

to whom we can provide mutual support. We must understand that marriage truly is ministry. Two people, equally yoked, become one spirit for the glory of God.

When two people are equally yoked in marriage, there is no tension in the links that bind them. The absence of tension means they can advance together in pursuit of God's purpose for their covenant. However, if one person moves ahead of the other, tension builds in the links, causing weakness in the marriage. If one spouse chooses to dig in his heels and resist forward advancement, it can cause the other to regress to relieve the tension, hindering the marriage's growth in God. The spouse advancing forward can pull along the lagging one as they advance, albeit slowly, due to the strain caused by the straggler. This, too, hinders them from fulfilling God's complete plan for their union.

God's instructions are for our good. He cautions us against unequally yoked marriages because of His infinite wisdom. God sees the heartache and destruction that lies ahead. He does not desire to withhold good things from His children. He wants you to have His very best and, therefore, warns you against relationships that will ultimately cause you heartache and destruction.

Toxic relationships are designed by the enemy to cause destruction. They bring imbalance to your life, throwing you off of the righteous living course God planned for you. You must break free from the toxic relationships that seek to deprive Christian women of righteous relationships with the Lord. Whether you are involved in or contemplating a relationship with an unbeliever while holding on to the hope that the man will change, know that God's warnings against such relationships are bathed in love. Heed God's admonition: Do not be unequally yoked (2 Corinthians 6:14)!

Bible students may want to remind me of the story of Hosea and Gomer (Hosea 1–3). God told Hosea, a great prophet of God, to marry Gomer, a woman who would become an adulterer. Hosea did as God instructed. Eventually, Gomer became just who God said she would become—an adulterer. Even so, God told Hosea to redeem and restore his wife. The key here is that Hosea had a sure Word from the Lord. Nevertheless, Hosea endured heartache and destruction in uniting with a woman who did not love the Lord. God had a purpose behind the union. He asked Hosea to sacrifice his life through such a union in order to teach a bigger lesson to His people. God made a modern day demonstration of how merciful He had been to Israel even though Israel committed adultery by serving other gods.

The life we live under the new covenant does not require mercy missions like the one involving Gomer and Hosea. The ultimate display of God's mercy was made when he removed Himself from Himself and became flesh, born of a woman. He lived, died, and was resurrected for our inheritance of eternal life. God extended Himself to us in sacrificial love. We responded by accepting His sacrifice and making Him Lord of our lives. Now we follow His commandments, allowing His will to be done through us in the earth as we enjoy the fruit of this life and await our transition into His heavenly kingdom.

Prayerful Application

Prayerfully consider God's Fatherly love extended toward you, His precious daughter. Consider why the loving Father admonishes His precious daughters to stay clear of known dangers. Receive God's love and pray for strength to obey God's admonitions.

Part III

Understand Your
Value to God

Chapter Seven

Do Not Settle for Less

> *For I know the thoughts that I think toward you, saith the LORD, thoughts of peace, and not of evil, to give you an expected end. Then shall ye call upon me, and ye shall go and pray unto me, and I will hearken unto you. And ye shall seek me, and find me, when ye shall search for me with all your heart. And I will be found of you, saith the LORD: and I will turn away your captivity, and I will gather you from all the nations, and from all the places whither I have driven you, saith the LORD; and I will bring you again into the place whence I caused you to be carried away captive.*
> Jeremiah 29:11–14

God loves you. He really does love you. He loves you so much that He sent His only begotten Son, Jesus, to live and die so that you would be saved (John 3:16). When you accepted Jesus as Lord and Savior, you became a precious daughter of the Most High God. You responded to God's sacrificial offering of His Son. Therefore, God responded with the gift of eternal life—eternal life that has already begun on earth as we await our transition into heaven.

God desires to bless you on earth. Although the reward of heaven is much to be desired, God wants to give you a glimpse of heaven on earth as He showers you with His goodness in response to your obedience. God desires that you have peace and prosperity in every aspect of your life, including relationships. A peaceful and prosperous relationship is one that is rich in love, commitment, communication, companionship, and provision. In peaceful and prosperous relationships, each person knows how to seek God, has the ability to hear from God, and strives to live according to God's perfect will.

Peaceful and prosperous relationships are made up of individuals who commit to being used by God to help their mates fulfill God's purpose for their lives. If God's purpose for you as a wife is that you work in the home, nurturing future prophets and world leaders, then your mate must commit to doing all that he can to free you from other cares. If God's purpose for your husband is that he be a giant financier for the church, then you must commit to doing all that you can to help him carry out God's plan. When God gives your husband a witty invention (Proverbs 8:12), you must be in a position to pray with him and help bring that vision to pass. Peaceful and prosperous relationships require selfless support of one another for God's glory.

If you choose to settle for the world's man, you reject God's plan for your life. Your actions suggest that you think you are better suited than God to give yourself what you think you need. Concerns about time cause many people to act prematurely. We want what we want when we want it. I hear you reasoning: "Lord, I'm 35 years old. If he has not come by now, he may never come. My reproductive clock is ticking and I'm running out of time to have children. He's a nice guy who will grow to love God over time. At least he has a good job and wants something out of life." You give yourself enough reasons to renounce the virtue of patience and set out on a course to help God do His job in your life.

God is your Creator, not you! God's wisdom defies the capabilities of the human mind. Your mind is incapable of perceiving the full plan God has for your life. *Now unto Him who is able to do exceeding abundantly above all that we ask or think, according to the power that worketh in us* (Ephesians 3:20). The human mind is limited. God wants to bless you beyond what the limited human mind can contemplate. God wants to bless you with a mate with whom you can unite as a part of His divine purpose. Marriage is ministry. God forms unions for His glory and so that His purpose can be fulfilled through the union. Because God forms unions for His glory and purpose, you must not intervene in God's plan, settling for less than what He has planned to give you.

We must learn to trust God in all things. As Christians, sometimes we find it easier to trust God in certain situations and not in others. We find it easy to trust God for the so-called easy things, such as providing us with food and shelter. When it comes to the seemingly hard things, such as the things that elude us—husbands, children, wealth—we step out of faith and into self-help. The problem with self-help in relationships is that you do not have complete knowledge of the future days God has planned for you. While you may be able to select a person to meet your present needs, only God has the insight to select a person who will meet your future needs. God knows what is forever best for us.

As my life continues to unfold, it bears witness to the fact that God knew what I needed in a husband. God used my brother Andrew to introduce my husband and me. That single introduction began what I pray will last a lifetime. How can I be so sure that our marriage will stand the test of time? We have invited Jesus to rule our marriage. Although we are prone to fail, our Lord and Savior does not fail.

I had my idea of the type of man I would marry. Having worked hard to be a successful attorney, I reasoned that he too had to be a professional who earned six figures. After all, I needed to have the option to exchange my title as employee and the daily stresses of long commutes for home-based entrepreneurship. He could not have children because I did not have the capacity for "baby mama drama." He had to have his own home in which we could live once married, because I intended to keep my home as my personal investment. And, of course, he had to love his family, community, and God as much as I did. Oh yeah, he had to be tall and handsome. My prayers were for what I thought was my type of man.

Prior to meeting Travis, I found peace in living as a single woman. I stopped complaining and accepted the fact that God would order my future husband's steps toward me in due season. In that season of my life, I came to the conclusion that God knew the desires of my heart and that, in fact, He had placed them there. He knew that I desired a husband. I resolved that I would wait on His timing.

At my brother's suggestion, Travis and I agreed to meet along with him and my sister Mary for an evening of bowling. In our initial meeting, I learned that Travis worked as a truck driver and had a six-year-old daughter. He owned a duplex that wasn't in the nicest part of town. He had many stories of how he had a strong relationship with God prior to being betrayed by someone who called himself a pastor. My score card indicated a deficit. However, as we continued to interact as friends, his love for his family became more evident. I watched him take care of his daughter and witnessed the exchange of mutual affection between his family members during gatherings at Big Ma's house.

I do not think I ever counted him out; I just never counted him in. He didn't measure up to the expectations I had; therefore, I didn't consider him as a future husband. As I learned more about him and shared more time with him developing a friendship, I began to see that his career, status as a "baby daddy," and seemingly cursory relationship with God didn't define the man. Those were tags I placed on him initially. God had given him designations that I could not see in the natural—designations that required spiritual insight. God called him "Mighty Man of God."

71

The truck driver is now a successful real estate sales agent and investor who helps afford me the blessing of working from home. Early in our marriage, God blessed Travis' minimal truck driver's salary and made it abundant with bonuses and commissions. His work was an example of what happens when you add God to the equation—extraordinary abundance. I did not have the foresight to see that God would transition Travis from driving trucks to handling lucrative real estate deals for our family as well as others. However, my spirit bore witness to the fact that he was a mighty man of God who loved God deeply. God blessed us with the benefit of prosperity without the trade-off of long commutes and excessive work hours, freeing us to be actively involved in ministry and community endeavors. God used Travis' duplex in what became a prime area to set the financial stage for our life together.

Although I escaped "baby mama drama," I encountered "baby drama" early in our relationship and into the early part of our marriage. My stepdaughter had a hard time sharing her father with me. In the flesh, that opposition was enough to drive me in the other direction. As God began to reveal to me that Travis would be my husband, I resisted because I could not handle the outward display of rejection exhibited by his daughter. But God began to show me that He had a plan for me in her life. While every detail of the plan has not been revealed to me, it has been enough for me to know that I am on an assignment from God to help her mother and father raise her to revere and live for God, and to expose her to many of life's opportunities. My assignment from God gives me courage to work toward being an effective stepparent as my stepdaughter begins to accept my role in her life.

As I maintained my life of devotion to God during the early stages of our relationship, Travis found his way back to an intimate relationship with God. I, too, began to call him by the name God had given him: "Mighty Man of God." Even though our union faces the challenges of two people living as one, undoubtedly, my husband is God's very best for me.

God is well able to give you the desires of your heart. Do not miss God's will for you because of packaging. Spiritual discernment is vital. Today's package may not be the packaging God wants to adorn him with in the future. However, if God promised you a knight in shining armor who works for corporate America earning six figures, lives in a mansion, does not have any children, and pastors a church, then wait for that promise. God is well able to present you to your "Mr. Right."

Know that if it is your heart's desire, God will present you to a man who loves God first and has the ability to love you second—that is, if you obey God. Trust God to provide you with a mate who lines up with God's Word. He will not be perfect because none of us is. He will be a man whose heart's desire is to please God. You will enjoy the benefit of that because the God-fearing man understands that it pleases God when he loves, protects, and provides for you as he should. Why settle for less than God's very best?

Prayerful Application

Ask God to minister to you concerning the type of man He has for you. If you are currently interested in someone or dating someone, ask God if he is God's very best for you.

Chapter Eight

Do Not Be Weary in Doing Well

And let us not be weary in well doing: for in due season we shall reap, if we faint not.
Galatians 6:9

Do you find yourself in toxic relationships because you have become weary while waiting on the Lord? Galatians 6:9 encourages us: *And let us not be weary in well doing: for in due season we shall reap, if we faint not.* You may have become weary doing the work of the Lord. You may wonder when your season of blessings will come. You feel yourself fainting, losing steam as you plow ahead in the Lord's vineyard. You try to muster the strength to encourage yourself in the Lord. "Press, persevere, run the race, stay the course, do not give up," I hear you whispering to yourself. In response, hear God encouraging you to not be weary in following His laws because, at the right time, you will reap the rewards of your obedience (Galatians 6:9).

God has given us the text of the Bible as His written instructions on how to live as Christians. As any good father would, He warns us against doing certain things to protect us. We must follow the instructions of the Holy Bible as we maneuver through life. For some, obedience comes easily, while others struggle to keep God's ordinances. Obedience becomes easier when we have a relationship with God. Our love for God requires more than a declaration of love and acceptance of Jesus Christ as Lord and Savior; it involves our actions. We should express our love to God by spending time with Him in prayer, talking to Him, and listening to Him. We spend time with those we love. We desire to please those we love. When we as followers of Jesus Christ love God with our whole being, we desire to please Him by obeying Him.

It is human nature to expect rewards for the good that we do. As children, we were rewarded with praise for our first steps, art projects, remembering our lines in the church's Easter play, and minding our manners. Oftentimes, the expected praise from our parents motivated us to do well. We learned as children that we could not always model the behavior of our parents, because their behavior was not always acceptable. Confusing though it was, many of us learned to obey the verbal instructions and weed through our parents' actions. They warned us: "Do as I say, not as I do."

Having mastered the art of doing as our parents said and not as they did when we were children, we enter adulthood with an Elder Brother, Jesus, who not only encourages us to do as He says, but to do as He did when He walked the earth as a man. In adulthood, we find ourselves choosing good actions because it is the right thing to do. We do good deeds because God said we should, and we want to be like our Elder Brother, Jesus, who lived as man, yet without sin. But human nature rises in us, and at times, if we are not careful, we can go back to childhood ways of thinking. We can take on the attitude that we will continue to do good deeds only if we are rewarded. Loving obedience results in God's blessings, while childish threats of disobedience close the windows of heaven.

The frustration mounts when we look around us and see our friends living what appear to be halfhearted lives for God, yet receiving the blessings of loving relationships and marriages, healthy children, successful careers, and prosperous businesses. This is where we mess up. God designed an individual course for each one of us. We cannot focus on a course designed by God for someone else. When we look at another's course, we run the risk of missing the directional signs God gives for our lives. God tells you to come here, but you go there because that's where your friend met her husband. God tells you to buy this, but you buy that because she has one and it seems to make her happy. God tells you to take this job, but you take that job because your friend who works there has had much success.

We must get to a place where we look to God for all counsel and direction. There is always more to the story than meets the eye when looking at someone else's course. What appears on the surface is not always the true heart of a matter. You may never know the extent of the challenges and struggles others have had to face to get where they are or to enjoy what they have in life. Also, you do not know whether they are walking in a blessing that will endure the test of time. Therefore, take your eyes off of everyone else and focus on God, your Creator—the One who sustains and provides for you.

In 2 Timothy 4, Paul talks about his Christian walk on earth as he awaits the reward of heaven. He writes: *For I am now ready to be offered, and the time of my departure is at hand. I have fought a good fight, I have finished my course, I have kept the faith: Henceforth there is laid up for me a crown of right-eousness, which the Lord, the righteous judge, shall give me at that day: and not to me only, but unto all them also that love his appearing* (2 Timothy 4:6–8).

Although Paul acknowledges that the crown that he seeks from the Lord is available to "them also that love [H]is appearing," he wrote about *his* journey toward the crown of righteousness. He said, "I have fought a good fight, I have finished my course, I have kept the faith." Paul finished *his* course, the course God ordained for him. Paul's course involved his conversion from a persecutor of Christians to a leader in Christianity.

For those who look upon Paul with envy because he was a chosen disciple of God, their envy is misplaced. They must know that he was also a persecutor and one who was persecuted. So it is in this world today. We must be careful not to desire the life that someone else has, because we may not be willing to endure the rigorous course that created the life they currently live. Know that God has a special course for you. We must focus on the course God has planned for us so that we, too, can declare at the time of our transition into the heavenly kingdom, "I have fought a good fight, I have finished *my* course, and I have kept the faith."

As you wait for the Lord to present you to your husband, continue to serve God with all of your heart, soul, and mind. In the book of Ruth, we learn that Ruth dedicated herself to following and helping her mother-in-law. God used Ruth's service to her mother-in-law to lead her on the course where she would meet Boaz, the wealthy man whom Ruth would eventually marry. As a single person, you are now free to concern yourself totally with pleasing the Lord (1 Corinthians 7:32). When you are married, in addition to pleasing God, you must please your husband (1 Corinthians 7:34). Embrace your season of singleness by devoting yourself to pleasing God primarily. Do not allow anyone to occupy space that should be reserved for God.

Do not grow weary; rather, celebrate this season in your life. Determine in your heart that you will not give way to weariness. Determine that you will trust God and attune yourself to walk the course He has designed for you, His special daughter.

If God has placed the desire for a husband in your heart, rest in faith knowing that you will reap if you faint not (Galatians 6:9). If God has called you to a life of singleness, rest in faith knowing that you will reap the rewards of living a single life of honor before God if you faint not.

Prayerful Application

In prayer, ask God for the spiritual strength you need to continue the course He has planned for you. Ask God to help you focus on Him and not on the courses of others. If you have become weary in doing good, ask God to give you a fresh revelation of His love for you and the plans that He has to bless you in this life.

Chapter Nine

You are a Gift *from* God; therefore, You Are Not Yours to Give

What? Know ye not that your body is the temple of the Holy Ghost which is in you, which ye have of God, and ye are not your own? For ye are bought with a price: therefore glorify God in your body, and in your spirit, which are God's.
1 Corinthians 6:19-20

I recall the mental tug of war I often encountered as I tried to justify being with someone who did not love the Lord as much as I did. The Spirit of the living God, who dwells in me, tugged me in the direction of walking away from the relationship because it did not please God. My flesh tugged me in the direction of giving the relationship a chance. "He's such a nice guy. He will change. He will someday accept Christ as Lord and Savior. Even if he does not make the commitment before marriage, then surely he will make the commitment once married," my flesh argued. As I sat contemplating whether it was worth taking a chance by committing myself to a man who was not a follower of Christ, the Lord spoke to me: "You are not yours to give."

Those six words changed my life: YOU ARE NOT YOURS TO GIVE. Case closed. The words reverberated in my head. Although I wanted to give myself to this man, God made it very clear that I could not give someone something that did not belong to me. You see, like me, you belong to the Lord. You are fearfully and wonderfully made (Psalm 139:14). God created you for His purpose. God has invested so much in you. He called you into His kingdom of eternal life. He called you into His kingdom of abundant blessings as a joint heir with Christ. You are His. God's ownership is written on your heart. Therefore, you cannot give something to someone that does not belong to you.

Someday, God will present you as a gift to a man of God who had enough faith to believe God for a queen. You will be his reward for honoring and obeying God. You will be his Deuteronomy 28 blessing (Deuteronomy 28:1–14). He will have been obedient to the Lord's commandments. You will be his reward, his prayer answered. Because you will be presented by the Lord as a gift, an answer to prayer, that man will thank God for you all the days of his life. But if you move ahead of God and present yourself as a gift to one undeserving of God's reward, you risk some-day being moved from the mantle where you were the center of the man's admiration to the attic with other items long forgotten.

My husband and I are both thankful that I did not give myself away, but that I allowed God to present me as a gift to my husband. When Travis appeared on the scene of my life, I had no idea that he would be my husband. My husband says he knew from our first encounter that I would be his wife, his gift from the Lord. Perhaps God did not reveal His plan to me because He wanted to present me as a gift to Travis rather than allow me to present myself. God knew that I had a record of attempting to give myself to men who were not in God's plan for my life. It did not become clear to me that I had met the one for whom I had prayed until a few months before he asked me to be his wife.

God showed me that He had chosen to present me as a gift to my husband. And I received a gift in return! God gave me Travis as my husband. We were each other's gift, given by our Heavenly Father who knows everything about us. We were given to each other by the Father who knew that we could learn to work together to create a marriage that would glorify Him. Our Father knew that we would have struggles in our marriage, and He knew that when the smoke cleared, we would manage to look with admiration upon each other as precious gifts from the Most High God.

There's something special about receiving a gift from God. So be patient. Don't be a woman who has named and claimed a man outside of God's will. You should not present yourself to a man who is not equipped to grow spiritually with you through the trials of life. If he does not perceive you as a gift from God, he may one day abuse and misuse you. If he sees himself as the gift, he may treat you as though he is doing you a favor by being with you.

There are many women who do not see themselves as the prize and, therefore, open the door to mistreatment. With time clocks ticking, they pursue men to ward off loneliness. They work hard, adorning themselves with fine linen, bathing themselves in precious perfumes, buying men expensive gifts, and stroking their egos in a quest to gain a husband. All too often, they win a man but lose out on gaining a true husband. Self-centered men are incapable of loving a woman as Christ loves the church because they do not know how Christ loves the church.

Allow God to present you as a gift. If you have given of yourself unworthily in a toxic relationship, it is not too late to renounce your part in the relationship. You were not yours to give in the first place. You are God's precious daughter. Let the Lord clean you up and restore you to fellowship with Him so that He can present you to the man He created for you.

Prayerful Application

Ask God to show you how to establish your worth in Him. Declare Psalm 139:14: *I will praise thee; for I am fearfully and wonderfully made: marvellous are thy works; and that my soul knoweth right well.* Assess the relationship you are in presently or the one you are contemplating. Are you the gift?

Part IV

Engage in Spiritual Warfare

Chapter Ten

Stand Guard against Satan's Devices

> *Finally, my brethren, be strong in the Lord, and in the power of his might. Put on the whole armour of God, that ye may be able to stand against the wiles of the devil. For we wrestle not against flesh and blood, but against principalities, against powers, against the rulers of the darkness of this world, against spiritual wickedness in high places. Wherefore take unto you the whole armour of God, that ye may be able to withstand in the evil day, and having done all, to stand.*
> Ephesians 6:10–13

It is important to recognize that walking away from a toxic relationship is not only a battle waged in the flesh, but it is a spiritual battle as well. The enemy of Christians' souls desires to destroy followers of Christ through toxic relationships.

Toxic relationships can draw us away from our relationship with God. They rob us of the blessings God intends for us to enjoy in healthy relationships. The enemy, who is after our souls and faith in God, will use destructive relationships to pull us away from our relationship with God. Saints of God, stand guard against Satan's devices. Demons are lurking in their quest to get you off course and destroy the future God has planned for you.

The person who does not believe in God is not your enemy. Because of sin, unbelievers and believers alike open doors in their lives that allow Satan, the Christian's chief enemy, to encourage them to behave in opposition to the teachings of Jesus Christ. A relationship with a Christian can also be toxic if the relationship is not designed by God.

Toxic relationships can hinder or delay the fulfillment of God's plan for your life. You were placed on this earth to do the will of the Father. There are exploits for His Kingdom that He desires done through you. There is ministry through music that must flow from your lips. There are teachings from His Word that will be made clear through you. There are end-time prophets that must come forth from your womb. There are houses of worship that will be built because of your generous giving. There are ministries that require your resources to reach the nations. When you are in a toxic relationship, the sin arising from that relationship prevents you from being fully available for God to orchestrate His will through you. Therefore, the toxic relationship becomes another god, exalted above the true and living God.

You must find strength to resist the enemy's devices. When you resist him, he will flee (James 4:7). Resisting the enemy involves warfare. Ephesians 6:13–18 instructs us in the preparation for warfare. Knowing that the enemy is in the earth to steal, kill, and destroy (John 10:10), you must prepare for battle. According to the Word of God, you must equip yourself with the whole armor of God for spiritual warfare. Ephesians 6:13–18 advises:

> *Wherefore take unto you the whole armour of God, that ye may be able to withstand in the evil day, and having done all, to stand. Stand therefore, having your loins girt about with truth, and having on the breastplate of righteousness; And your feet shod with the preparation of the gospel of peace; Above all, taking the shield of faith, wherewith ye shall be able to quench all the fiery darts of the wicked. And take the helmet of salvation, and the sword of the Spirit, which is the word of God: Praying always with all prayer and supplication in the Spirit, and watching thereunto with all perseverance and supplication for all saints.*

Truth is a key part of your armor. Truth always wins when faced with lies and deceit. Truth remains a constant, while lies and deception are exposed as the story changes over time. In resisting the devil, it is important for you to trust God's Word to combat the attacks of the enemy. As you trust God's Word, you must walk in its truths.

Further, you must hide the Word of God in your heart so that you won't sin against God (Psalm

119:11). Therefore, righteousness is the breastplate that shields your heart. Righteousness is living a life modeled after God's Word. Righteousness is not reserved for church settings or among people of God; righteousness must be a way of life, an embodiment of the life of Jesus Christ. You must trust in the power of the living God to teach you to defeat the enemy. God, the Living Water, dashes the flames of the enemy.

Moreover, the gospel of peace and the shield of faith are vital parts of the armor needed in the war against the enemy. When you are confident in God, you can exist in peace even in the middle of the battlefield. You are to take and carry peace with you wherever you go. *Peace I leave with you, my peace I give unto you: not as the world giveth, give I unto you. Let not your heart be troubled, neither let it be afraid* (John 14:27). You can exist in peace, recognizing that even though you have been called to the battlefield against Satan and his cohorts, the actual battle belongs to the Lord (1 Samuel 17:47). The shield of faith allows you to stand in the den of lions like Daniel, yet know that God will not allow you to be devoured (Daniel 6:10–23). We can declare with the Bible writer Paul:

> *But we have this treasure in earthen vessels, that the excellency of the power may be of God, and not of us. We are troubled on every side, yet not distressed; we are perplexed, but not in despair; Persecuted, but not forsaken; cast down, but not destroyed; Always bearing about in the body the dying of the Lord Jesus, that the life also*

of Jesus might be made manifest in our body. (2 Corinthians 4:7–10)

Also, our salvation and God's Word are mighty shields for the battleground. There is no room for fear when you engage in battle knowing that you will not die because you have been given eternal life as a result of your salvation. *And these shall go away into everlasting punishment: but the righteous into life eternal* (Matthew 25:46). There is no room for fear in spiritual warfare because the Word of God declares your victory. *Ye shall not need to fight in this battle: set yourselves, stand ye still, and see the salvation of the LORD with you, O Judah and Jerusalem: fear not, nor be dismayed; to morrow go out against them: for the LORD will be with you* (2 Chronicles 20:17).

Once you are fully armored, you must exercise your spiritual authority as a joint heir with Christ (Galatians 4:7). Stand your ground against the devil and his cohorts under the power of the Holy Ghost (Matthew 12:28).

Stand guard over your heart. Protect yourself from the onslaught of the enemy's devices to bind you through toxic relationships. Protect yourself by offering praise and worship to God. When you praise and worship God, you remind yourself of the sheer goodness and awesomeness of God. In praising Him, you connect with God's power, empowering you to tread on the enemy's head.

Stand guard over God's will for your life. God created you to glorify Him in every aspect of your life. Protect yourself from toxic relationships that distract you from pursuing God's will for your life. Protect yourself by studying the Word of God. Set aside time to study God's Word, which contains His love notes and words of encouragement to you, His beloved. The Bible offers guidance for living a life that is pleasing to God. God wants the very best for you. Line up all relationships with God's Word. If the relationship is not a part of God's will for your life, ask God for the strength to release it.

Stand guard over your faith in God. The disappointments of life can gnaw away at your faith if you are not careful. Do not deal with disappointing times by seeking your own solutions to problems rather than looking to God for the answers. Protect your faith in God by holding fast to God's promises despite disappointments. Resist Satan through fasting unto God. Isaiah 58:8–12 declares the benefits of fasting:

Then shall thy light break forth as the morning, and thine health shall spring forth speedily: and thy righteousness shall go before thee; the glory of the LORD shall be thy reward. Then shalt thou call, and the LORD shall answer; thou shalt cry, and he shall say, Here I am. If thou take away from the midst of thee the yoke, the putting forth of the finger, and speaking vanity; And if thou draw out thy soul to the hungry, and satisfy the afflicted soul; then shall thy light rise in obscurity, and thy darkness be as the noonday: And the LORD shall guide thee continually, and satisfy thy soul in drought, and make fat thy bones: and thou shalt be like a watered garden, and like a spring of water, whose waters fail not. And they that shall be of thee shall build the old waste places: thou shalt raise up the foundations of many generations; and thou shalt be called, The repairer of the breach, The restorer of paths to dwell in.

Stand guard over your witness for Christ. Christians are the salt of the earth (Matthew 5:13). Living righteously in all aspects of your life, including relationships, glorifies God. Others may be drawn to your God when they see the reward you receive for living righteously before Him. So that you do not spoil your witness for God, you must resist Satan through prayer. Through prayer, you will find the spiritual strength you need to resist toxic relationships. When you spend quality time in the presence of God, you are strengthened to resist the devil's traps. You must fellowship with your Creator in continuous song and prayer. Love on God without ceasing. Press into the Lord to understand His ways. Let Jesus Christ be your model as you live with a transformed mind in this world (Romans 12:2).

Prayerful Application

In prayer, ask God for strength to resist Satan. In the name of Jesus, renounce Satan's devices operating against your life. Commit to resisting Satan's devices through praise and worship, studying the Holy Scriptures, fasting, and praying.

Chapter Eleven

Do Not Allow Your Flesh to Hinder You

But I keep under my body, and bring it into subjection: lest that by any means, when I have preached to others, I myself should be a castaway.
1 Corinthians 9:27

Human beings are comprised of spirit, soul, and body (1 Thessalonians 5:23). Once you are born again as a Christian, you must live out your salvation through the conviction in your soul, guided by your spirit, while suppressing the will of your flesh. The Holy Scriptures instruct us:

> *There is therefore now no condemnation to them which are in Christ Jesus, who walk not after the flesh, but after the Spirit* (Romans 8:1); *That the righteousness of the*

97

law might be fulfilled in us, who walk not after the flesh, but after the Spirit (Romans 8:4); *For if ye live after the flesh, ye shall die: but if ye through the Spirit do mortify the deeds of the body, ye shall live.* (Romans 8:13)

The desire to live righteously for God is developed deep within the soul. The Holy Spirit then comes in and connects with your eternal spirit to help you fulfill your deep longing to live righteously for God. The flesh rebels as you become more God-centered, recognizing that its self-centered days are nearing an end.

When you feed your spirit man by studying God's Word, praying, and fasting, you grow in the love, grace, knowledge, and power of God. However, your domineering flesh will try to work against you to destroy you. *This I say then, Walk in the Spirit, and ye shall not fulfil the lust of the flesh* (Galatians 5:16). Therefore, to enjoy your inheritance as a joint heir with the Lord, you must crucify the desires of the flesh.

Like Paul, you should commit yourself to live for God and declare: *But I keep under my body, and bring it into subjection: lest that by any means, when I have preached to others, I myself should be a castaway* (1 Corinthians 9:27). A spirit-led life attracts unbelievers to God (Matthew 5:16). A Christian's life, driven by the flesh, repels people from the very God the Christian professes. You do not want to be guilty of hindering another's relationship with God because they see you living a life of sin.

In some instances, the enemy will try to destroy you by resurrecting your past defeats. Sex is one of the greatest challenges that many Christians face in relationships. Sex is a key trap the enemy uses to entice believers into sin. Even when you've been set free from sexual sins, the familiar spirits of fornication, adultery, masturbation, lust, and/or perversion may reappear if you have dealt with them in the past. Such temptations are Satan's attempt to entice you back into sin. If you continue to resist sexual temptations, the devil will flee (James 4:7). However, if you entertain the temptations, you will walk into Satan's trap.

Make a decision to be led by the Holy Spirit. Allow your spirit man to dominate your flesh. A life led by the Holy Spirit leads to abundance. Choose to live by the instructions received by your inner spirit from the Holy Spirit. Do not allow your flesh to hinder you.

When you enter into relationships with people who do not share your spiritual values, it can become even more difficult to resist the temptation to fall into sexual sin. Fornication seems to present the greatest challenge for single Christians. Although the Bible forbids premarital sex (1 Corinthians 6:18), the world encourages sex outside of marriage. Therefore, if you, a Christian, engage in sexual activity outside of marriage, you must deal with the guilt of fornication. On the other hand, an unbeliever is usually unaffected emotionally by the sexual encounter because he or she does not feel accountable to living righteously for God. Thus, the conflict arises.

The unbeliever explains that sex is his soulful

expression of intense love toward you. He does not know how to express the love of God because he does not understand God's expression of love. God's love is born of the Spirit, not of the flesh. You must not fall into the trap of accepting his expression of love—love born of the flesh, not of the Spirit. Hold out for the type of love expressed by God.

Even so, some Christians find themselves receptive to sexual advances or initiating sexual contact because of the desire to please their flesh above pleasing the Spirit of God. They find themselves in this predicament because of the things they have allowed to enter their spirits, such as sexually explicit television shows or movies, girl talk with unsaved friends, or improper physical contact with the opposite sex. A disciplined life in God requires you to bring the desires of the flesh into subjection to the truths of God so that you won't be a poor witness for Jesus Christ (1 Corinthians 9:27).

Our God is a loving God who forgives us of our sins. Through repentance, we can cast down and renounce our sins. True repentance creates a renewed mind set toward doing God's will. When we repent, God forgives us, cleanses us, and makes us pure (1 John 1:9). Although God forgets our sins, satanic spirits lurk around, trying constantly to condemn us for our past sins. We have a weapon against Satan. When condemning thoughts come, we are to cast them down and acknowledge the acceptance of God's forgiveness (2 Corinthians 10:4, 5; Romans 8:1).

Yielding to the flesh can hinder your relationship with God. Jill and Scott met and married after only six months of dating. They claimed to have known from the very beginning that they were to be married. One of the reasons that they planned to marry so quickly was because of sexual temptation.

Jill, who was a virgin, had committed her life to celibacy. Having been raised by parents who were missionaries, she had been a follower of Christ since she was a young girl. Scott, on the other hand, was a Christian struggling with illicit sex demons from his past. Scott had recently become a Christian. Prior to meeting Jill, he had been a womanizer, regularly engaging in sex with many different women. By the power of God, Scott had been willing to walk away from his sex driven lifestyle and begin his pursuit of a relationship with God.

Jill and Scott met at a church sponsored singles event. They began going out on dates with other singles and married couples, but soon separated themselves from groups and began to spend time together. Scott told Jill how much he loved her and desired to have her as his wife. His flesh began to rise up, reminding him of how he expressed "love" in the past. He tried to convince Jill to have sex with him. At first, Jill refused.

Early one morning, they found themselves in a compromising situation. Jill found the strength to resist Scott yet again. Afterwards, they prayed together. Scott, wanting to live righteously in His new walk with God, decided that it was better that they marry rather than sin (1 Corinthians 7:9). They married a few weeks later, much to the disappointment of their pastor and Jill's parents. Six months after they married, Scott found himself unfulfilled sexually and struggling to resist the temptation of adultery. In their situation, the flesh drove the union. They answered the flesh's cry for satisfaction without undergoing the counseling and deliverance needed prior to marriage.

Walking away from a potentially toxic relationship is not always easy, but it is necessary. Build up your spirit man through the study of God's Word, praying, and fasting. Do not allow your flesh to destroy you. Recognize that during this season of singleness, you are free to devote more of your time to serving God (1 Corinthians 7:34). Rely upon the power of God to give you strength to pull yourself away from involvement in a toxic relationship or the thought of getting into a toxic relationship. Also, ask God to direct you to someone you can trust to hold you accountable to do the right thing. Although the battle with the flesh is strong, you can be victorious with the power of God (Philippians 4:13). God's power manifests in our lives when we renew our minds with the Word of God and submit to being led by the Holy Spirit (Galatians 5:16). The Word of God contains the power to overcome.

Prayerful Application

Pray that God will reveal to you areas of your life being controlled by your flesh, rather than by the Holy Spirit living in you. Find Scriptures that relate to the areas you are being challenged in and meditate on them to renew your mind. Pray God's Word back to Him, claiming every promise for yourself. Renounce Satan's influence in your life. Confess your sins, and declare your resolve to live a Spirit-led life.

Part V

Commune with Your God

Chapter Twelve

Tell God How You Really Feel

> *Call unto me, and I will answer thee,*
> *and shew thee great and mighty*
> *things, which thou knowest not.*
> Jeremiah 33:3

There is no such thing as hiding your feelings from God. Our God is omniscient. While your words and actions may tell one story, God knows the things imbedded in your heart. Stop fooling yourself and others, and tell God how you really feel. You may ask, "If God knows what is on my heart, then why is there a need for me to tell Him?" God, our Creator, wants to communicate with His creation—you! He wants you to reach out to Him with the issues of your heart. Jeremiah 33:3 declares: *Call unto me, and I will answer thee, and shew thee great and mighty things, which thou knowest not.* God promises to tell you great and mighty things to help you through your situation, but there is a prerequisite: God says, "Call unto me." When you call Him, He answers.

Our Christian walk should involve fellowship with God. Our triune God is not only our Father and Elder Brother, He has extended Himself to us as a comforter, a friend. A true friend is someone in whom you can confide your most treasured thoughts without the fear of them being revealed to others. A true friend is a cheerleader, one who encourages you to be your very best, cheering you along as you reach toward your goals. A true friend listens. A true friend is your sounding board, the one who listens to your point of view without judging you, yet lovingly offers advice in response. Jesus is the best friend one can ever have. After you have confided in Him, be open to hear the constructive criticism of a dear friend who also happens to be your sovereign God.

You must be real with God. Tell Him how you feel about the man you say you love. Tell God about the struggle you have with releasing this man although you know in your heart that he is not dedicated to living for the Lord. Tell God that you are struggling because, even though he has not accepted Jesus as his personal Savior, he is a loving and caring man. Tell God that you have the faith to believe Him for that man's conversion to Christianity. Your reasoning is that it is okay to share your life with this man now because someday he will change. Tell God that you believe you can handle the risk of loving a man who does not love God because this man is so wonderful in all other ways. Tell the Lord that unless He provides you with a God-fearing man who has accepted and submitted himself to the lordship of

Christ Jesus, you will die. Be true. Tell God how you really feel. Hannah told God how she felt.

Hannah desired to have a son, yet she was barren. In *bitterness of soul*, Hannah prayed and cried out to the Lord (1 Samuel 1:10). She cried out in such despair that the priest mistook her passion and desperation for drunkenness (1 Samuel 1:11–15). *And Hannah answered and said, No, my lord, I am a woman of sorrowful spirit: I have drunk neither wine nor strong drink, but have poured out my soul before the Lord... for out of the abundance of my complaint and grief have I spoken* (1 Samuel 1:15–16). Hannah got God's attention as well as the attention of the man of God.

In life, we often wear different masks to shield others from seeing the true us. During periods of great pain, we learn to suck it up and put on our "everything is fine" mask. We wear this mask in front of our co-workers or fellow church members in an effort to keep them out of our personal affairs. We get so comfortable wearing masks that we forget to take them off when we enter our prayer chambers. We offer masked prayers to God as though He does not know our hearts. We bless God in word, but our hearts are far from true praise because of the pain of a situation with which we struggle. Hannah reached a point where she could no longer bear the pain of being barren and teased because of her condition.

Hannah reached a point where she tore off her "everything is fine" mask and displayed the sheer ugliness of her pain. She cried out to God with such emotion that the priest assumed that she had to be intoxicated.

Like Hannah, you must become vigilant about what you desire from God. It is okay to desire a healthy relationship that leads to marriage. You may find it difficult to petition God for a mate when you compare your request to those of people in need of healing, food, shelter, and finances for basic needs. You might question: "How dare I petition God for a husband when there are people around me with far greater needs?" Indeed, God is well able to hear all of the prayers of his children and answer them all without delay. Remember, Abba Father (Galatians 4:6) is sovereign.

Hannah became outwardly honest about the suffering she had endured silently. Oftentimes we suffer silently because we are afraid to acknowledge the strong desire for a particular thing at the risk of seeming ungrateful for the things God has already given us and the things He has done for us. Although Hannah was barren, she was so beloved by her husband that he gave her double provision in comparison to what he gave to his other wife and children (1 Samuel 1:5). Having been a good provider and caregiver to Hannah, her husband initially could not understand why she wanted more. *Then said Elkanah her husband to her, Hannah, why weepest thou? and why eatest thou not? and why is thy heart grieved? am not I better to thee than ten sons?* (1 Samuel 1:8).

There may be people in your life asking a question similar to the one Hannah's husband asked of her. They ask, "Aren't you satisfied with the blessings you have?" They say, "You have a great job, a nice place to live, and supportive friends. You are financially stable and active in a growing and powerful church ministry, yet you long for a God-filled marriage." Others look at your total situation and call you ungrateful. You must look to your God, knowing that He is well able to bless you with the God-given desires of your heart (Psalm 20:4). Hannah pulled on the priest. She pulled on God. She pulled on them out of desperation for an answer to her prayers, knowing that only God could bless her with a son.

Hannah vowed to God that she would return unto Him the very gift (her son) for whom she had petitioned (1 Samuel 1:11). *And she said, Oh my lord, as thy soul liveth, my lord, I am the woman that stood by thee here, praying unto the LORD. For this child I prayed; and the LORD hath given me my petition which I asked of him: Therefore also I have lent him to the LORD; as long as he liveth he shall be lent to the LORD. And he worshipped the LORD there* (1 Samuel 1:26– 28). Are you willing to give God the very relationship you desire?

You give God the relationship by allowing Him to be glorified through the relationship. People should be drawn to God by how you live out the many aspects of your life, including relationships with the opposite sex. Live righteously. *Let not then your good be evil spoken of* (Romans 14:16). Give God the relationship by choosing to obey Him whether He confirms the relationship or reveals that it is not His perfect will for you. Just as Hannah gave her answered prayer (her son, Samuel) to God for God's glory, you must be willing to give your relationship to God for God's glory. Do not offer God a toxic relationship.

Prayerful Application

Go to God in prayer, and confess the real issues of your heart. Cry out to Him for help with the challenges in your life. Be honest with Him.

Chapter Thirteen

Hear God's Response
to Your Struggles

> *For we have not an high priest which cannot be touched with the feeling of our infirmities; but was in all points tempted like as we are, yet without sin.*
> Hebrews 4:15

God loves you. God loves you. You, God loves! You are His precious daughter. Just as you long for the desires of your heart, He longs to give you those desires (Psalm 21:2). After all, He is the originator of all righteous desires in your heart. God not only knows the struggles of living in the world, but He understands your struggles because of His own suffering. *For we have not an high priest which cannot be touched with the feeling of our infirmities; but was in all points tempted like as we are, yet without sin* (Hebrews 4:15). Now that you have shared your heart with God, hear God's response through His Word.

God loves you. He loves you so much that He offered His very own Son, Jesus, to die so that you would receive the promise of eternal life (John 3:16). Having made such a great sacrifice for you by presenting His Son to die, God does not want Satan to prevail in your life. God paid a price for you; therefore, He wants you to choose to live for Him. As you strive to live for God, beware of the desperately wicked heart that can lead you astray. God wants you to line up your emotions with His Word. If the Holy Scriptures forbid you from being unequally yoked, then do not allow your heart and your emotions to rationalize your involvement in a relationship with an unsaved man.

God wants to bless you with not only the spiritual love He gives to His children. God wants to also express His love physically through a mate (Genesis 2:18-23). God modeled the institution of marriage after Christ's relationship with the church. God wants you to have the very best. God wants you to have a relationship that leads to a marriage filled with the type of sacrificial love He expresses toward His children. But how can an unsaved man love you as Christ loves the church if he does not know how Christ loves the church? God's laws are not intended to hinder you but to bless you.

God forgives you of your sins. Do not allow condemnation to overwhelm you. The sooner you accept God's love and His forgiving grace, the sooner you will begin your journey to deliverance. We all have sinned and fallen short of the glory of God, but God extends forgiveness and mercy. We need only repent—turn our hearts and minds away from sin—and receive His hand of mercy. Your repentance is a matter you can control. Just as God does not control the will of a person, you cannot control the will of a man.

Therefore, use this time to focus on developing your relationship with God. God is glorified when you live for Him, causing others to take note and inquire about the blessings they see manifested in your life. Pray for others so that they may come to the saving knowledge of Jesus Christ as Lord and Savior. You cannot force a person's hand in the matter. Nor can you forsake your obedience to Christ for the sake of a relationship.

God wants you to run the race He has predestined for you, no matter how difficult it may seem. God wants the very best for you. He wants to shield you from harm and cause you to prosper in all things, including relationships. God is cheering you on, encouraging you to continue to obey Him. He is encouraging you to continue to run life's race without getting weary. Press your way to obedience. You are a precious gift to be given only by your Creator, the God of the universe. God wants to present you as a gift. Let Him do it.

The enemy of your soul opposes your desire to live in obedience to God's Word. However, God has given you His Word as ammunition in your war against Satan. Put on the armor of God so that you can withstand the attacks of the enemy. Renounce all of Satan's devices to lead you away from right-eousness. Feed your spirit man and starve your flesh so that you can have a toxin-free, victorious relation-ship.

Once you have expressed how you feel about the situation you are facing, God responds with love. He wants you to know that He loves you. He desires your love in return. *If ye love me, keep my com-mandments* (John 14:15).

Prayerful Application

Prayerfully, make the following confessions: God loves me so much that He gave His beloved Son to die so that I could have eternal life (John 3:16). I will not allow my heart to be deceived into engag-ing in relationships that are contrary to the will of God (Jeremiah 17:9). I accept God's forgiving grace for the wrongs I have done in the past (Psalm 86:5). I will wait on the manifestation of a healthy relationship in which my mate is growing or has grown to love me with the sacrificial love Jesus Christ has for His people (Ephesians 5:25; 2 Co-rinthians 6:14). I will not get weary in serving God because I know that I will receive the promise of His blessings, including prosperity and a good fu-ture (Galatians 6:9; 3 John 1:2).

Part VI

Embrace Your Freedom

Chapter Fourteen

Make a Decision to Walk in God's Truth

> *For the Lord GOD will help me; therefore shall I not be confounded: therefore have I set my face like a flint, and I know that I shall not be ashamed.*
> Isaiah 50:7

Once the truth of God's Word is revealed to us, we must make a decision to walk in God's truth. God loves us so much that He reveals His will for our lives in many different ways. God's Word, the Holy Bible, is the sure message for our hearts. Although He can and does speak to us by His Spirit, the flesh can interfere with the reception of God's message if we are not totally grounded in God. Therefore, when in doubt, we must judge a situation by the Word of God.

We must line up our actions with the understanding of God's will (James 4:17; James 1:22). Oftentimes, we know God's truths in our minds. However, God wants us to know His truths in our hearts so that we won't sin against Him. To walk in victory, we must bridge the gap between *knowing* God's truths and *obeying* God's truths.

In the first section of the book, you were challenged to review your existing or contemplated relationship for signs of toxicity. In part two, you were encouraged to face the realities of the impending heartache that generally accompanies toxic relationships. You were encouraged to consider the question: How can he love me as Christ loves the church if he does not know how Christ loves the church?

The third section of this book implored you to embrace the fact that God loves you so very much. Only God can offer you as a gift. In the fourth section, you were encouraged to resist the enemy of your soul and die to your flesh in pursuit of obedience to God. In the fifth section, you were encouraged to open up to God and tell Him the matters of your heart.

Now it is time for you to embrace your freedom. When Christ Jesus sets you free, you are free indeed (John 8:36). Now is the time to make a decision for the Lord. Today is decision day. Choose this day whom you will serve (Joshua 24:15). If it be God, then serve God by ridding yourself of toxic relationships. If it be Baal, then know that our merciful God is also a God of judgment (1 King 18:21). Obedience is better than sacrifice (1 Samuel 15:22). It is your choice to make.

Jesus made a choice for us. He had a choice to submit to death on a cross to redeem man or allow us to lapse into eternal damnation. He had a choice. Yes, it was the Father's will that He die that we might live, but Jesus chose to obey God and submit to death on a cross. He had a choice. The fact that Jesus had a choice was evidenced in the garden of Gethsemane. With a heart filled with anguish, Jesus said, "O my Father, if it be possible, let this cup pass from me: nevertheless not as I will, but as thou wilt" (Matthew 26:39). He had a choice.

I imagine that Jesus could have chosen to abandon His assignment. Yet the love He had for the Father caused Him to submit to the will of the Father. Jesus submitted to God's will being done through Him. Jesus was very aware that the will of the Father meant His physical death. Although He faced the agony of the cross, Jesus made a decision to do the will of the Father. He suppressed His flesh and chose the will of His Father. *For we have not an high priest which cannot be touched with the feeling of our infirmities; but was in all points tempted like as we are, yet without sin* (Hebrews 4:15). As a Christian woman seeking deliverance from toxic relationships, you can find strength by looking to your Elder Brother, Jesus.

At some point in the journey toward total deliverance from toxic relationships, I developed a "made up mind." I made up my mind to serve the Lord with all my heart, soul, and mind. I followed the Lord's leading out of toxic relationships and received His great protection from shame (Isaiah 50:7). I focused intensely on the things of God, setting my face like a flint (hard rock) (Isaiah 50:7). I closed the door to distractions. I embraced the freedom God had already given me.

I do not suggest that it was a simple process, but it was a process in which I relied on God's strength when I was weak. I received God's Word as instructions for pleasing God and living a victorious life through Christ Jesus. I had a choice to make. I could please God and receive the blessings of His eternal provisions, or I could please my flesh and receive merely momentary gratification.

Today is decision day. Make a decision to walk in God's truth. Pray and ask God for wisdom on how to exit your toxic relationship. Do not allow the fear of finances and loneliness to stagnate you. Give your fears to God and allow Him to order your steps out of the toxic relationship and into a God-ordained relationship.

Prayerful Application

Prayerfully, write a decision-day letter to God. Tell God about your decision to live for Him and glorify Him in every aspect of your life, including relationships.

Chapter Fifteen

Rise Up, Daughter of Abraham, and Dress in Your Royal Garments

> *And who knoweth whether thou art come to the kingdom for such a time as this?"*
> Esther 4:14

You must come to terms with who you really are as you embrace your deliverance from toxic relationships. Knowing your lineage should inspire you to live victoriously for God. Among your many titles is "Daughter of Abraham." As a daughter of Abraham, you are an heir to the promises God made to Abraham and his lineage.

God told Abraham that he would be a father of

many nations (Genesis 17:4). God made a covenant with Abraham that He would not only be Abraham's God but the God of the generations that would flow from Him (Genesis 17:7). God promised Abraham that nations and kings would come from him (Genesis 17:6). We, the daughters of Abraham, are the "kings" promised to Abraham by the Almighty God. Kings and kingdoms are established through inheritance. We partake in the inheritance of Abraham through acceptance of the shed blood of Jesus Christ who redeemed us from our sins (Galatians 3:6-7,13-14).

As believers, we must be open to receive our entitlement as heirs of God's covenant with Abraham. We are entitled to such blessings because we are daughters of Abraham. The thirteenth chapter of Luke reveals how a fellow daughter of Abraham received healing from Jesus Christ because of God's covenant with Abraham:

> *And he was teaching in one of the synagogues on the sabbath. And, behold, there was a woman which had a spirit of infirmity eighteen years, and was bowed together, and could in no wise lift up herself. And when Jesus saw her, he called her to him, and said unto her, Woman, thou art loosed from thine infirmity. And he laid his hands on her: and immediately she was made straight, and glorified God. And the ruler of the synagogue answered with indignation, because that Jesus had healed on the sabbath day, and said unto the people, There are six days in which men ought to*

work: in them therefore come and be healed, and not on the sabbath day. The Lord then answered him, and said, Thou hypocrite, doth not each one of you on the sabbath loose his ox or his ass from the stall, and lead him away to watering? And ought not this woman, being a daughter of Abraham, whom Satan hath bound, lo, these eighteen years, be loosed from this bond on the sabbath day? And when he had said these things, all his adversaries were ashamed: and all the people rejoiced for all the glorious things that were done by him. (Luke 13:10–17)

The Lord stepped out of the tradition established by the religious leaders of that day. He saw a daughter of Abraham existing outside of the promise His Father, God, made to her spiritual father, Abraham. He reached out to help her receive the promises of God. The Lord released her from the tormenting spirit of infirmity, freeing her to walk in the healing promised to the heirs of Abraham.

After delivering the woman from bondage, Jesus asked: *And ought not this woman, being a daughter of Abraham, whom Satan hath bound, lo, these eighteen years, be loosed from this bond on the sabbath day?* (Luke 13:16). Ought not we, who have been bound by toxic relationships, be loosed to experience relationships that line up with God's Word? Indeed, we ought.

Accept your position as a daughter of Abraham. Allow the God of Abraham, Isaac, and Jacob to be your God (Exodus 3:15). In addition to reaping the

123

benefits of your lineage, glorify God with your life so that others will be drawn to your God. You are a highly favored daughter of the God of Abraham, Isaac, and Jacob. Now it is time to add your name to that great lineage. Let your life declare that He is the God of Abraham, Isaac, Jacob, and _____.

(add your name here)

God wants to replace the ashes from the destructive fires that raged in your life because you failed to douse them with the Word of God, fasting, and prayer. Gather the ashes from toxic relationships. God wants to give you beauty in exchange for those ashes (Isaiah 61:3). God wants to give you beauty that will glorify Him, beauty that flows through your spirit. As you come to terms with the fact that you are indeed a precious daughter of the Most High God, the beauty God created in you from the time He placed you in your mother's womb will come forth. Rise up, oh daughter of Abraham, and dress in your royal garments!

Accept the call of God upon your life. He has destined you for greatness in Him. Walk out your greatness in God as you live a life that glorifies Him and draws others to a relationship with your God.

Esther answered the call. The book of Esther in the Holy Scriptures chronicles the fall of one queen and the elevation of another so that the will of God would be done in the earth. So it is with each of us, my sisters. God wants to elevate us to a place where He can use us for His glory.

Esther, a Jewish woman, was chosen queen after Queen Vashti was dethroned for disobedience to King Ahasuerus. Esther's quest to become the queen was

God-ordained: God gave Esther favor with the chamberlain, who ensured that she would be prepared to compete to be King Ahasuerus' queen. God blessed her to earn a position of honor so that He could use that position to bring glory to Him and protect the Jewish people against destruction. Based on deceptive information and unaware of his queen's heritage, King Ahasuerus issued a decree that all Jewish people be put to death.

Queen Esther, herself a Jewish woman, was subject to the king's decree unless she found the boldness required to confront the king. As Esther struggled with self-doubt, her adoptive father, Mordecai, challenged her: *And who knoweth whether thou art come to the kingdom for such a time as this?* (Esther 4:14). Mordecai, who raised Esther as his very own daughter after her parents died, pushed Esther toward her destiny.

Esther, once an orphan, had been strategically positioned to thwart the enemy's plans against the people of God. She is a testament that we should not allow negative things from our past to dictate our future. Dressed in her royal garments, Esther went before King Ahasuerus and petitioned him for the deliverance of the Jews from the death decree he had issued. Having found favor with the king, she won the security of her people. As Mordecai suggested, indeed Esther had been made queen for such a time as to ensure the security of God's people.

As daughters of the Most High God and the seed of God's beloved Abraham, dress in your royal garments and embrace healthy relationships that are in line with God's plan for your life.

Prayerful Application

Prayerfully, ask God to reveal to you the plans He has for your life to glorify Him. Let the Holy Spirit reveal to you the past events of your life that have helped mold you for God's call on your life. Exchange the ashes of past sin and disappointment for God's beauty. Dress in your royal garments and surrender to God so that He can dispatch you on your next mission designed for His glory.

Chapter Sixteen

Praise Your Way
to Deliverance

> *Make a joyful noise unto the LORD, all ye lands. Serve the LORD with gladness: come before his presence with singing. Know ye that the LORD he is God: it is he that hath made us, and not we ourselves; we are his people, and the sheep of his pasture. Enter into his gates with thanksgiving, and into his courts with praise: be thankful unto him, and bless his name. For the LORD is good; his mercy is everlasting; and his truth endureth to all generations.*
> Psalm 100

Although you are on the last leg of the journey toward deliverance or protection from toxic relationships, it can be just the beginning of a renewed love affair with God. By now, you know in your heart whether the relationship you are in or the one you're contemplating is toxic. Prayerfully, you have made up your mind to choose God's course for your life, refusing to allow the enemy to impede you through toxic relationships.

The psalmists in the Holy Scriptures learned to praise God through the most challenging situations in their lives. Through their praise, the psalmists found favor with God. Since God is not a respecter of persons (Acts 10:34), we can confidently emulate the psalmists in praising our way through to deliverance.

Psalm 116 chronicles a thankful song of worship from one whom God spared from death. Let's apply this psalm of thanksgiving as you receive God's loving deliverance from toxic relationships--past, present, and future. Psalms 116 reads:

> *I love the LORD, because he hath heard my voice and my supplications. Because he hath inclined his ear unto me, therefore will I call upon him as long as I live. The sorrows of death compassed me, and the pains of hell gat hold upon me: I found trouble and sorrow. Then called I upon the name of the LORD; O LORD, I beseech thee, deliver my soul. Gracious is the LORD, and righteous; yea, our God is merciful. The LORD preserveth the simple: I was brought low, and he helped me. Return unto thy rest, O my soul; for the LORD hath dealt bountifully with thee. For thou hast delivered my soul from death, mine eyes from tears, and my feet from falling. I will walk before the LORD*

in the land of the living.

I believed, therefore have I spoken: I was greatly afflicted: I said in my haste, All men are liars. What shall I render unto the LORD for all his benefits toward me? I will take the cup of salvation, and call upon the name of the LORD. I will pay my vows unto the LORD now in the presence of all his people. Precious in the sight of the LORD is the death of his saints. O LORD, truly I am thy servant; I am thy servant, and the son of thine handmaid: thou hast loosed my bonds. I will offer to thee the sacrifice of thanksgiving, and will call upon the name of the LORD. I will pay my vows unto the LORD now in the presence of all his people, In the courts of the LORD'S house, in the midst of thee, O Jerusalem. Praise ye the LORD.

As daughters of God, we have the privilege of talking directly to our Father. God welcomes us to call upon Him at all times. God must be number one in our lives. When we depend on God, He shows up mightily in our lives, showering us with His grace and mercy as He helps us live victoriously on the earth. Although our earthly reward cannot be compared with our heavenly reward, we can enjoy God's presence in the land of the living. Call upon God and offer him the sacrifice of thanksgiving as you receive your deliverance from toxic relationships.

Prayerful Application

Offer Psalm 116 as an earnest prayer to God in the name of Jesus Christ. Know that you have been brought into the Kingdom of God to fulfill your divine purpose. Do not allow anyone or anything to get in your way.

Closing

As God ministered His response to my cry, "I love him Lord, but he's not a Christian," I began to truly understand that God's instructions were designed to work a far greater good in my life than I could ever imagine. God knows what is best for His children. As Christians who are called to operate in faith, we must do the will of God even when it does not feel good to the flesh. Faith says, "God, I trust you." We show our trust in God when we obey Him. His Word cautions us against yoking ourselves with unbelievers. It is best that we obey God fully in all aspects of our lives; sacrifices are poor substitutes for obedience in the parts of our lives we want to control. *To obey is better than sacrifice* (1 Samuel 15:22). Saul learned this valuable lesson.

In 1 Samuel 15:1–26, God speaks through the prophet Samuel to Saul concerning the consequences of Saul's disobedience. The Lord told Samuel to anoint Saul king over Israel. In preparation for Saul's first battle as king, God gave Saul specific instructions concerning the destruction of the Amalekites. God ordered Saul to destroy the Amalekites and all their belongings. However, Saul and his fellow warriors spared the king of the Amalekites and preserved some of the Amalekites' best livestock and other goods. God had ordered the destruction of it all. Saul's disobedience caused God to remove him as king.

When Samuel confronted Saul concerning the spoils that had been taken from the war, Saul explained that he and the people took the best livestock to offer as a burnt offering to God. *And Samuel said, Hath the LORD as great delight in burnt offerings and sacrifices, as in obeying the voice of the LORD? Behold, to obey is better than sacrifice, and to hearken than the fat of rams. For rebellion is as the sin of witchcraft, and stubbornness is as iniquity and idolatry. Because thou hast rejected the word of the LORD, he hath also rejected thee from being king* (1 Samuel 15:22–23).

Rather than obey God's order to destroy the Amalekites and all of their goods, Saul took spoils and attempted to offer some of the Amalekites' goods to God as a sacrifice. Saul tried to appease God by offering a sacrifice rather than giving God what He requested—obedience.

God does not accept substitutions for obedience. Therefore, it is better that you obey God's admonition against being unequally yoked. It is better to reject toxic relationships rather than offer God justifications for existing in toxic relationships. God wants you to have His very best. Do not settle for less. The call that God has on your life is at stake. Just as Esther was called into God's kingdom to do a work for God, you have been called for a special work. Seek God for revelation concerning the work He has prepared for you.

Let God's love be perfected in you, my dear sister. Although you may "love" a man who is not God's best for you, love God more as you resolve to reject toxic relationships. After all, how can he love you as Christ loves the Church if he does not know how Christ loves the church?

Prayer of Deliverance

Dear God,

Thank you for the gift of salvation through your Son, Jesus Christ. Thank you for loving me enough to show me the way to live victoriously in the relationship You have destined for me. I pray that I will be strengthened to show my love for you through obedience.

I renounce all toxic relationships. Father, I choose to deny my flesh and follow the leading of the Holy Spirit in my relationship. I receive the deliverance from toxic relationships you freely give me. Thank you Father for giving me the strength and wisdom to guard my heart against those who are unable to love me as Christ loves the church.

In the name of Jesus, the Christ, I pray. Amen.

Prayer of Salvation

Although many of you who have read this book are Christians, I recognize that some of you may not be. Therefore, I offer this prayer to you as an invitation to join the family of believers in Jesus Christ. Christians may use this prayer as a confession of their faith and rededication of their life to Jesus Christ.

Dear God,

I come to you acknowledging that I am a sinner (Romans 3:23). Forgive me of my sins and cleanse my heart of all unrighteousness.

Thank you for loving me so much that You gave Your only Son, Jesus, to die on a cross so that I could have eternal life (John 3:16).

I confess with my mouth and believe in my heart that Jesus died, You raised Him from the dead, and He still lives (Romans 10:9). I accept Jesus as my Lord and Savior and receive Your gift of salvation (Romans 5:8, 18).

In the name of Jesus, the Christ, I pray. Amen.

I Love Him Lord,[TM] *but He's Not a Christian*
Order Form

Please Print:

Name_____

Address_____

City_____ **State** _____ **Zip**_____

Phone_____

_____copies of book @ $12.00 each	$_____
Florida residents add sales tax	$_____
Postage and handling @ $2.00 (1-2 books), $3.00 (3-4 books), $4.00 (5-9 books)	$_____
Total amount enclosed	$_____

(Contact us for postage and handling costs and discount book rates for orders of 10 books or more.)

Make checks payable to Jewel Publishers, LLC

Send to Jewel Publishers, LLC
P. O. Box 278006
Miramar, FL 33027

www.jewelpublishers.com
admin@jewelpublishers.com

Speaking Engagement Inquiry Form

Use this convenient form to inquire about Latasha Hines' availability to speak to church, civic, charitable, book club, and professional groups.

Please Print:

Name_____

Address_____

City_____ **State** _____ **Zip**_____

Phone_____

Proposed Date and Time _____

Event _____

Theme _____

Program Format _____

_____

Comments _____

Send to Jewel Publishers, LLC
P. O. Box 278006
Miramar, FL 33027

www.jewelpublishers.com
admin@jewelpublishers.com